The One Lamp That Lights The Worlds

A translation of

THE AVADHŪTA GĪTĀ

OF DATTĀTREYA

Anonymous

Anonymous may be contacted at
songoftheavadhuta@gmail.com

To

Him

Whose Grace Alone

Lights the Lamp in our Hearts

Preface

I wish I had an exciting story to tell – a story of revelation, magic, and mystery. But the only mysteries I know are life itself – a mystery at every turn, and God, who is mystery and magic, and hopefully one day, revelation as well.

Mine is an everyday tale. One night I was surfing the web and came across the Avadhūta Gītā. As I started to read it, I was mesmerized, turned to my husband, and said, "I've found my true calling in life – it's the study of Advaita texts!" I was familiar with Hindu Scripture, but no text had fascinated me as much as the Aṣṭāvakra Saṁhitā, which I had translated the previous summer, and now the message of the Avadhūta captivated me. The message is so direct and linear, there's nothing more to think about, or to add. In the words of Aṣṭāvakra, "There is No More to Say!"

The Message

It's a Phantasmagoria!

The Only Constant is You!!

The Conclusion

It's not fair! :)
My silhouette gets to play
While I do Nothing!

My silhouette gets to enjoy
To frolic
To win .... to lose
To teach .... to learn
To love .... to be loved
To be joyous .... to be sad
To live and to die

And I?
Beyond Living and Dying, Bondage and Freedom
Unborn and Unchanging, Pure and Perfect
Consciousness, Ever Luminous and All-Infusing
One Indivisible Continuum
Indistinguishable from the Supreme
Beyond Duality and Non-Duality
The Innate Reality
The One Absolute Truth, All and Entire
The One Singular Truth of All Existence

So who was the Avadhūta?

And who was Dattātreya?

The Avadhūta is a liberated soul who has achieved the highest state of spiritual realization. Beyond renunciation and acceptance, aim and aimlessness, free of the chains of hope, the norms of conduct, of Everything, "He is the Absolute - Pure and Perfect."

Dattātreya, born as the son of Atri and Anasūyā, was the Lord of the Avadhūtas. He was the incarnation of Viṣṇu. Anasūyā was granted a boon by the gods. She wanted Brahmā, Viṣṇu, and Śiva to be born as her sons. Her wish was granted and Brahmā was born as Soma, Viṣṇu as Dattātreya, and Śiva as Durvāsā.

In beautiful Sanskrit poetry, the sage describes his direct experience of Truth. He makes no philosophical arguments but spontaneously professes the Ultimate Reality in sublime asservations. The reader is elevated from darkness unto light, from illusion unto knowledge, from sorrow unto bliss, and from bondage unto freedom.

Contents

Chapter 1: You are the Most Supreme Truth 1
Chapter 2: The Perfect One Is The Lord of the Universe! 77
Chapter 3: The Whole is Eternal and Non-Eternal......... 117
Chapter 4: The Wise drink of the Nectar of Renunciation 163
Chapter 5: Truth lies Beyond the Absolute and the Relative 189
Chapter 6: There is No Distinction between Cause and Effect 221
Chapter 7: He is the Absolute - Pure and Perfect........... 249
Chapter 8: He lives in A State of Eternal Bliss 265
Other Books by the Same Author 277

Chapter 1

You are the Most Supreme Truth

1.1

ईश्वरानुग्रहादेव पुंसामद्वैतवासना ।
महद्भयपरित्राणाद्विप्राणामुपजायते ॥

īśvarānugrahād-eva puṁsām-advaita-vāsanā,
mahadbhaya-paritrāṇād-viprāṇām-upajāyate.

The Grace of God Alone
Kindles yearning for The One Reality,
Removing the dread
In plurality and death.

1.2

येनेदं पूरितं सर्वमात्मनैवात्मनात्मनि ।
निराकारं कथं वन्दे ह्यभिन्नं शिवमव्ययम् ॥

yena-idaṁ pūritaṁ sarvam-ātmanaivā-ātmanā-ātmani,
nirākāraṁ kathaṁ vande hy-abhinnaṁ śivam-avyayam.

The Universe is Fully Suffused by the Self,
And the Self Solely Exists.
How then could I, who am the Self, worship mySelf –
Auspicious, Formless, Unchanging, and Impartible?

1.3

पञ्चभूतात्मकं विश्वं मरीचिजलसन्निभम् ।
कस्याप्यहो नमस्कुर्यामहमेको निरञ्जनः ॥

pañcabhūtātmakaṁ viśvaṁ marīci-jala-sannibham,
kasyāpy-aho namas-kuryām-aham-eko nirañjanaḥ.

This Universe of Five Elements
Is Delusive like the Waters of a Mirage.
To whom would I offer obeisance,
I, the Immaculate One?

1.4

आत्मैव केवलं सर्वं भेदाभेदो न विद्यते ।
अस्ति नास्ति कथं ब्रूयां विस्मयः प्रतिभाति मे ॥

ātmaiva kevalaṁ sarvaṁ bhedābhedo na vidyate,
asti nāsti kathaṁ brūyāṁ vismayaḥ pratibhāti me.

The Self Singularly is All,
Beyond Distinction and Non-Distinction.
How would I avouch its Existence or Non-Existence?
Wonderstruck am I!

1.5

वेदान्तसारसर्वस्वं ज्ञानं विज्ञानमेव च ।
अहमात्मा निराकारः सर्वव्यापी स्वभावतः ॥

vedānta-sāra-sarvasvaṁ jñānaṁ vijñānam-eva ca,
aham-ātmā nirākāraḥ sarvavyāpī svabhāvataḥ.

The Soul of the Vedas,
Of all Knowledge and Wisdom, is this:
I am the Self, Formless and All-Pervasive,
By My Very Own Nature.

1.6

योो वै सर्वात्मको देवो निष्कलो गगनोपमः ।
स्वभावनिर्मलः शुद्धः स एवाहं न संशयः ॥

yo vai sarvātmako devo niṣkalo gaganopamaḥ,
svabhāva-nirmalaḥ śuddhaḥ sa evāhaṁ na saṁśayaḥ.

That One God who is the Self of All,
Undivided like the Sky,
Pure and Sinless by His Nature,
Is Undeniably who I am.

1.7

अहमेवाव्ययोऽनन्तः शुद्धविज्ञानविग्रहः ।
सुखं दुःखं न जानामि कथं कस्यापि वर्तते ॥

aham-evāvyayo'nantaḥ śuddha-vijñāna-vigrahaḥ,
sukhaṁ duḥkhaṁ na jānāmi kathaṁ kasyāpi vartate.

Verily I am the Immutable Infinite,
Of the form of Pure Knowledge.
Transcending Joy and Sorrow,
I am oblivious of how and whom they afflict.

1.8

न मानसं कर्म शुभाशुभं मे
न कायिकं कर्म शुभाशुभं मे ।
न वाचिकं कर्म शुभाशुभं मे
ज्ञानामृतं शुद्धमतीन्द्रियोऽहम् ॥

na mānasaṁ karma śubhāśubhaṁ me
na kāyikaṁ karma śubhāśubhaṁ me,
na vācikaṁ karma śubhāśubhaṁ me
jñānāmṛtaṁ śuddham-atīndriyo'ham.

I transcend Mental Activity, Good and Evil.
I transcend Physical Activity, Good and Evil.
I transcend Verbal Activity, Good and Evil.
Transcending the Senses, I am Pure.
I am Amrita, the Nectar of Knowledge!

1.9

मनो वै गगनाकारं मनो वै सर्वतोमुखम् ।
मनोऽतीतं मनः सर्वं न मनः परमार्थतः ॥

mano vai gaganākāraṁ mano vai sarvato-mukham,
mano'tītaṁ manaḥ sarvaṁ na manaḥ paramārthataḥ.

The Mind is of the form of Space,
Still, it dons Innumerable faces.
It dwells in the Past, and Everywhere,
Yet, it is not the Supreme Truth.

1.10

अहमेकमिदं सर्वं व्योमातीतं निरन्तरम् ।
पश्यामि कथमात्मानं प्रत्यक्षं वा तिरोहितम् ॥

aham-ekam-idaṁ sarvaṁ vyomātītaṁ nirantaram,
paśyāmi katham-ātmānaṁ pratyakṣaṁ vā tirohitam.

I am One and I am All,
Beyond Space, and Infinite.
How should I perceive myself,
As the Unmanifest or the Manifest?

1.11

त्वमेवमेकं हि कथं न बुध्यसे
समं हि सर्वेषु विमृष्टमव्ययम् ।
सदोदितोऽसि त्वमखण्डितः प्रभो
दिवा च नक्तं च कथं हि मन्यसे ॥

tvam-evam-ekaṁ hi kathaṁ na buddhyase
samaṁ hi sarveṣu vimṛṣṭam-avyayam,
sadodito'si tvam-akhaṇḍitaḥ prabho
divā ca naktaṁ ca kathaṁ hi manyase.

You too are the One! How can you not see that?
The Same Unchanging Light, Shimmering in Everyone!
The Ever-Luminous, All-Infusing Effulgence,
Outshining night and day!

1.12

आत्मानं सततं विद्धि सर्वत्रैकं निरन्तरम् ।
अहं ध्याता परं ध्येयमखण्डं खण्ड्यते कथम् ॥

ātmānaṁ satataṁ viddhi sarvatraikaṁ nirantaram,
ahaṁ dhyātā paraṁ dhyeyam-akhaṇḍaṁ khaṇḍyate katham.

Know the Self as One, Continuous, Everywhere.
You say I am the Meditator,
And the Supreme the Object of Meditation,
Why do you divide the One Undividable Whole?

1.13

न जातो न मृतोऽसि त्वं न ते देहः कदाचन ।
सर्वं ब्रह्मेति विख्यातं ब्रवीति बहुधा श्रुतिः ॥

na jāto na mṛto'si tvaṁ na te dehaḥ kadācana,
sarvaṁ brahmeti vikhyātaṁ bravīti bahudhā śrutiḥ.

You are never born, nor do you ever die,
Nor are you ever the body.
It is well-known that All is Brahman.
Scripture has declared this in diverse ways.

1.14

स बाह्याभ्यन्तरोऽसि त्वं शिवः सर्वत्र सर्वदा ।
इतस्ततः कथं भ्रान्तः प्रधावसि पिशाचवत् ॥

sa bāhyābhyantaro'si tvaṁ śivaḥ sarvatra sarvadā,
itastataḥ kathaṁ bhrāntaḥ pradhāvasi piśācavat.

You are That which is both Outside and Inside.
You are Auspicious, Eternal, and All-Imbuing.
Why then are you so misguided,
Running around like a ghost?

1.15

संयोगश्च वियोगश्च वर्तते न च ते न मे ।
न त्वं नाहं जगन्नेदं सर्वमात्मैव केवलम् ॥

saṁyogaśca viyogaśca vartate na ca te na me,
na tvaṁ nāhaṁ jagan-nedaṁ sarvam-ātmaiva kevalam.

There is neither Union nor Separation for You,
Nor for Me.
There is neither You, nor I, nor the World.
All is the Self Alone.

1.16

शब्दादिपञ्चकस्यास्य नैवासि त्वं न ते पुनः ।
त्वमेव परमं तत्त्वमतः किं परितप्यसे ॥

śabdādi-pañcakasyāsya naivāsi tvaṁ na te punaḥ,
tvameva paramaṁ tattvam-ataḥ kiṁ paritapyase.

You do not belong to the World of the Senses,
Nor does the World belong to You.
You are the Ultimate Truth.
Why then do you grieve?

1.17

जन्म मृत्युर्न ते चित्तं बन्धमोक्षौ शुभाशुभौ ।
कथं रोदिषि रे वत्स नामरूपं न ते न मे ॥

janma mṛtyuh-na te cittaṁ bandha-mokṣau śubhāśubhau,
kathaṁ rodiṣi re vatsa nāma-rūpaṁ na te na me.

For you, there is neither Birth nor Death nor Mind,
Bondage nor Liberation, Good nor Evil.
Why then, Dear Child, do you cry?
You and I have neither Name nor Form.

1.18

अहो चित्त कथं भ्रान्तः प्रधावसि पिशाचवत् ।
अभिन्नं पश्य चात्मानं रागत्यागात्सुखी भव ॥

aho citta kathaṁ bhrāntaḥ pradhāvasi piśācavat,
abhinnaṁ paśya cātmānaṁ rāga-tyāgāt-sukhī bhava.

O Mind, why do you stray confused
Like a ghost?
Know the Indivisible Self,
Relinquish Attachment, and be Happy!

1.19

त्वमेव तत्त्वं हि विकारवर्जितं
निष्कम्पमेकं हि विमोक्षविग्रहम् ।
न ते च रागो ह्यथवा विरागः
कथं हि सन्तप्यसि कामकामतः ॥

tvameva tattvaṁ hi vikāra-varjitaṁ
niṣkampam-ekaṁ hi vimokṣa-vigraham,
na te ca rāgo hyathavā virāgaḥ
kathaṁ hi santapyasi kāma-kāmataḥ.

Verily, you are the Timeless Truth,
Immutable, Immovable, One,
Of the Nature of Freedom.
You have neither Attachment nor Aversion,
Why then do you suffer by yielding to desire?

1.20

वदन्ति श्रुतयः सर्वाः निर्गुणं शुद्धमव्ययम् ।
अशरीरं समं तत्त्वं तन्मां विद्धि न संशयः ॥

vadanti śrutayaḥ sarvāḥ nirguṇaṁ śuddham-avyayam,
aśarīraṁ samaṁ tattvaṁ tanmāṁ viddhi na saṁśayaḥ.

Scripture proclaims Reality as
Attribute-less, Pure, Inextinguishable,
Bodiless and Equally Existent in All.
Know Yourself as this Truth, beyond all doubt!

1.21

साकारमनृतं विद्धि निराकारं निरन्तरम् ।
एतत्तत्त्वोपदेशेन न पुनर्भवसम्भवः ॥

sākāram-anṛtaṁ viddhi nirākāraṁ nirantaram,
etat-tattvopadeśena na punar-bhava-sambhavaḥ.

Know Form to be Falsity
And the Formless Eternal.
One who lives this Truth
Escapes the cycle of birth and rebirth.

1.22

एकमेव समं तत्त्वं वदन्ति हि विपश्चितः ।
रागत्यागात्पुनश्चित्तमेकानेकं न विद्यते ॥

ekam-eva samaṁ tattvaṁ vadanti hi vipaścitaḥ,
rāga-tyāgāt-punaḥ-cittam-ekānekaṁ na vidyate.

Reality is One and the Same,
The Sages declare that.
When Attachment is Relinquished
The mind no longer questions Unity or Duality.

1.23

अनात्मरूपं च कथं समाधि-
रात्मस्वरूपं च कथं समाधिः ।
अस्तीति नास्तीति कथं समाधि-
र्मोक्षस्वरूपं यदि सर्वमेकम् ॥

anātma-rūpaṁ ca kathaṁ samādhiḥ
ātma-svarūpaṁ ca kathaṁ samādhiḥ,
astīti nāstīti kathaṁ samādhiḥ
mokṣa-svarūpaṁ yadi sarvam-ekam.

If we think we are other than the Self,
How is that realization?
If we think we are the Self,
How is that realization?
If we think that the Self exists and also does not exist,
How is that realization?
Realization is Seeing Everything as One!

1.24

विशुद्धोऽसि समं तत्त्वं विदेहस्त्वमजोऽव्ययः ।
जानामीह न जानामीत्यात्मानं मन्यसे कथम् ॥

viśuddho'si samaṁ tattvaṁ videhas-tvam-ajo'vyayaḥ,
jānāmīha na jānāmīt-yātmānaṁ manyase katham.

You are the Pure, Homogenous Reality,
Beyond Body, Birth, and Death.
How can you say, I know the Self,
Or, I do not know the Self?

1.25

तत्त्वमस्यादिवाक्येन स्वात्मा हि प्रतिपादितः ।
नेति नेति श्रुतिर्ब्रूयादनृतं पाञ्चभौतिकम् ॥

tattvamasyādi-vākyena svātmā hi pratipāditaḥ,
neti neti śrutir-brūyāt-anṛtaṁ pāñca-bhautikam.

The saying, "That Thou Art"
Asserts the reality of your true Self.
The saying, "Not this, Not this"
Negates the reality of the five elements.

1.26

आत्मन्येवात्मना सर्वं त्वया पूर्णं निरन्तरम् ।
ध्याता ध्यानं न ते चित्तं निर्लज्जं ध्यायते कथम् ॥

ātmany-evātmanā sarvaṁ tvayā pūrṇaṁ nirantaram,
dhyātā dhyānaṁ na te cittaṁ nirlajjaṁ dhyāyate katham.

The Self is the Identity of All.
You are Whole, Immanent and Impartible.
The Meditator and the Meditation do not exist in you,
How then can you go on meditating unabashedly!

1.27

शिवं न जानामि कथं वदामि
शिवं न जानामि कथं भजामि ।
अहं शिवश्चेत्परमार्थतत्त्वं
समस्वरूपं गगनोपमं च ॥

śivaṁ na jānāmi kathaṁ vadāmi
śivaṁ na jānāmi kathaṁ bhajāmi,
ahaṁ śivaś-cet-paramārtha-tattvaṁ
sama-svarūpaṁ gaganopamaṁ ca.

I do not know Śiva, how would I speak of Him?
I do not know Śiva, how would I worship Him?
I am Śiva, the Truth of All.
Ever the Same, like the Sky.

1.28

नाहं तत्त्वं समं तत्त्वं कल्पनाहेतुवर्जितम् ।
ग्राह्यग्राहकनिर्मुक्तं स्वसंवेद्यं कथं भवेत् ॥

nāhaṁ tattvaṁ samaṁ tattvaṁ
kalpanā-hetu-varjitam,
grāhya-grāhaka-nirmuktaṁ
svasaṁvedyaṁ kathaṁ bhavet.

"I am not Truth, I am same as Truth,"
Free of such whimsical thoughts,
Free of the notions of Perceiver and Perceived,
How can I behold myself as an object?

1.29

अनन्तरूपं न हि वस्तु किंचि-
त्तत्त्वस्वरूपं न हि वस्तु किंचित् ।
आत्मैकरूपं परमार्थतत्त्वं
न हिंसको वापि न चाप्यहिंसा ॥

ananta-rūpaṁ na hi vastu kiṁcit
tattva-svarūpaṁ na hi vastu kiṁcit,
ātmaikarūpaṁ paramārtha-tattvaṁ
na hiṁsako vāpi na cāpy-ahiṁsā.

There is no object which is of Infinite form.
There is no object of Real form.
The Self Alone is the Supreme Reality.
It is neither violent nor the source of violence.

1.30

विशुद्धोऽसि समं तत्त्वं विदेहमजमव्ययम् ।
विभ्रमं कथमात्मार्थे विभ्रान्तोऽहं कथं पुनः ॥

viśuddho'si samaṁ tattvaṁ
videham-ajam-avyayam,
vibhramaṁ katham-ātmārthe
vibhrānto'haṁ kathaṁ punaḥ.

You are the Pure, Homogenous Truth.
You are Bodiless, Birth-less, and Indestructible.
How can there be delusion for you?
How can the Self be deluded?

1.31

घटे भिन्ने घटाकाशं सुलीनं भेदवर्जितम् ।
शिवेन मनसा शुद्धो न भेदः प्रतिभाति मे ॥

ghaṭe bhinne ghaṭākāśaṁ sulīnaṁ bheda-varjitam,
śivena manasā śuddho na bhedaḥ pratibhāti me.

When the pot is broken
Pot space merges with Infinite Space.
So also, when the mind is purified
It merges with Infinite Reality and perceives not Duality.

1.32

न घटो न घटाकाशो न जीवो जीवविग्रहः ।
केवलं ब्रह्म संविद्धि वेद्यवेदकवर्जितम् ॥

na ghaṭo na ghaṭākāśo na jīvo jīva-vigrahaḥ,
kevalaṁ brahma saṁviddhi vedya-vedaka-varjitam.

There is neither pot nor pot space,
Neither jiva nor body.
Know that there is only the One Brahman,
Beyond Knower and Known.

1.33

सर्वत्र सर्वदा सर्वमात्मानं सततं ध्रुवम् ।
सर्वं शून्यमशून्यं च तन्मां विद्धि न संशयः ॥

sarvatra sarvadā sarvam-ātmānaṁ satataṁ dhruvam,
sarvaṁ śūnyam-aśūnyaṁ ca tanmāṁ viddhi na saṁśayaḥ.

Everywhere, Always, and in Everything,
The Self Alone Exists - Unchangeably and Eternally.
Everything, Non-Existence, and Existence are both my Self.
I know this without doubt.

1.34

वेदा न लोका न सुरा न यज्ञा
वर्णाश्रमो नैव कुलं न जातिः ।
न धूममार्गो न च दीप्तिमार्गो
ब्रह्मैकरूपं परमार्थतत्त्वम् ॥

vedā na lokā na surā na yajñā
varṇāśramo naiva kulaṁ na jātiḥ,
na dhūma-mārgo na ca dīpti-mārgo
brahmaikarūpaṁ paramārtha-tattvam.

There are no Vedas, no Worlds, no Gods, and no Sacrifices.
No life stages, lineage, or caste.
Neither the path of smoke nor the path of light.
There is Only Brahman, the Supreme Reality.

1.35

व्याप्यव्यापकनिर्मुक्तः त्वमेकः सफलं यदि ।
प्रत्यक्षं चापरोक्षं च ह्यात्मानं मन्यसे कथम् ॥

vyāpya-vyāpaka-nirmuktaḥ tvam-ekaḥ saphalaṁ yadi,
pratyakṣaṁ cāparokṣaṁ ca hyātmānaṁ manyase katham.

When you have known the One,
Beyond Pervader and Pervaded,
How can you think of the Self
As Perceptible or Imperceptible?

1.36

अद्वैतं केचिदिच्छन्ति द्वैतमिच्छन्ति चापरे ।
समं तत्त्वं न विन्दन्ति द्वैताद्वैतविवर्जितम् ॥

advaitaṁ kecid-icchanti dvaitam-icchanti cāpare,
samaṁ tattvaṁ na vindanti dvaitādvaita-vivarjitam.

Some seek Non-Duality,
While others seek Duality.
Neither knows the Undifferenced Truth,
Beyond both Duality and Non-Duality.

1.37

श्वेतादिवर्णरहितं शब्दादिगुणवर्जितम् ।
कथयन्ति कथं तत्त्वं मनोवाचामगोचरम् ॥

śvetādi-varṇa-rahitaṁ śabdādi-guṇa-varjitam,
kathayanti kathaṁ tattvaṁ manovācām-agocaram.

It is free of Colors such as white,
And Qualities such as sound.
What can one say about the Truth,
Which lies beyond Mind and Speech?

1.38

यदाऽनृतमिदं सर्वं देहादिगगनोपमम् ।
तदा हि ब्रह्म संवेत्ति न ते द्वैतपरम्परा ॥

yadā'nṛtam-idaṁ sarvaṁ dehādi-gaganopamam,
tadā hi brahma saṁvetti na te dvaita-paramparā.

When you know the Body and the Universe
To be Unreal, and Empty like the Sky,
Then you truly know Brahman.
Then the practice of Duality ceases to exist.

1.39

परेण सहजात्मापि ह्यभिन्नः प्रतिभाति मे ।
व्योमाकारं तथैवैकं ध्याता ध्यानं कथं भवेत् ॥

pareṇa sahajātmāpi hya-bhinnaḥ pratibhāti me,
vyomākāraṁ tathaivaikaṁ dhyātā dhyānaṁ kathaṁ bhavet.

I perceive my Innate Self
As Indistinguishable from the Supreme,
As One Continuum, like Space.
How then can there be meditator and meditation
As two separate entities?

1.40

यत्करोमि यदश्नामि यज्जुहोमि ददामि यत् ।
एतत्सर्वं न मे किंचिद्विशुद्धोऽहमजोऽव्ययः ॥

yat-karomi yad-aśnāmi yaj-juhomi dadāmi yat,
etat-sarvaṁ na me kiṁcit-viśuddho'ham-ajo'vyayaḥ.

What I do, what I eat, sacrifice, or give,
Is not at all mine.
I am Pureness Itself,
Unborn and Unchanging.

1.41

सर्वं जगद्विद्धि निराकृतीदं सर्वं जगद्विद्धि विकारहीनम् ।
सर्वं जगद्विद्धि विशुद्धदेहं सर्वं जगद्विद्धि शिवैकरूपम् ॥

sarvaṁ jagad-viddhi nirākṛtīdaṁ
sarvaṁ jagad-viddhi vikāra-hīnam,
sarvaṁ jagad-viddhi viśuddha-dehaṁ
sarvaṁ jagad-viddhi śivaikarūpam.

Know the Entire Universe to be Without Form.
Know the Entire Universe to be Without Change.
Know the Entire Universe to be Pure Brahman.
Know the Entire Universe to be of the Nature of Śiva.

1.42

तत्त्वं त्वं न हि सन्देहः किं जानाम्यथवा पुनः ।
असंवेद्यं स्वसंवेद्यमात्मानं मन्यसे कथम् ॥

tattvaṁ tvaṁ na hi sandehaḥ kiṁ jānāmi-athavā punaḥ,
asaṁvedyaṁ svasaṁvedyam-ātmānaṁ manyase katham.

You are the Ultimate Truth, there is no doubt.
Otherwise, what do I know?
The Self knows the Self.
How can you believe it is Unknowable?

1.43

मायाऽमाया कथं तात छायाऽछाया न विद्यते ।
तत्त्वमेकमिदं सर्वं व्योमाकारं निरञ्जनम् ॥

māyā-amāyā kathaṁ tāta chāyā-achāyā na vidyate,
tattvam-ekam-idaṁ sarvaṁ vyomākāraṁ nirañjanam.

Child, how can there be Illusion and Non-illusion?
Shadow and Non-Shadow?
All this is the One Truth,
All-Pervasive and Flawless.

1.44

आदिमध्यान्तमुक्तोऽहं न बद्धोऽहं कदाचन ।
स्वभावनिर्मलः शुद्ध इति मे निश्चिता मतिः ॥

ādi-madhyānta-mukto'haṁ na baddho'haṁ kadācana,
svabhāva-nirmalaḥ śuddhaḥ iti me niścitā matiḥ.

Free in the beginning, middle and end,
I have never been bound.
My nature is Pure and Perfect.
This is My Conviction.

1.45

महदादि जगत्सर्वं न किंचित्प्रतिभाति मे ।
ब्रह्मैव केवलं सर्वं कथं वर्णाश्रमस्थितिः ॥

mahad-ādi jagat-sarvaṁ na kiṁcit-pratibhāti me,
brahmaiva kevalaṁ sarvaṁ kathaṁ varṇā-śrama-sthitiḥ.

I do not perceive this Whole Universe
Or the Cosmic Intelligence.
All is Brahman Alone.
Where then are caste or the stages of life?

1.46

जानामि सर्वथा सर्वमहमेको निरन्तरम् ।
निरालम्बमशून्यं च शून्यं व्योमादिपञ्चकम् ॥

jānāmi sarvathā sarvam-aham-eko nirantaram,
nirālambam-aśūnyaṁ ca śūnyaṁ vyomādi-pañcakam.

I know Everything as the One, Uninterrupted Reality,
Self-Shining and Full.
While the five elements
Such as ether, are empty.

1.47

न षण्ढो न पुमान्न स्त्री न बोधो नैव कल्पना ।
सानन्दो वा निरानन्दमात्मानं मन्यसे कथम् ॥

na ṣaṇḍho na pumānna strī na bodho naiva kalpanā,
sānando vā nirānandam-ātmānaṁ manyase katham.

The Self is neither neuter, nor masculine, nor feminine.
Neither an understanding nor imagination.
How then can you think
The Self is blissful or not blissful?

1.48

षडङ्गयोगान्न तु नैव शुद्धं मनोविनाशान्न तु नैव शुद्धम् ।
गुरूपदेशान्न तु नैव शुद्धं स्वयं च तत्त्वं स्वयमेव बुद्धम् ॥

ṣaḍaṅga-yogānna tu naiva śuddhaṁ
manovināśān-na tu naiva śuddham,
gurūpadeśān-na tu naiva śuddhaṁ
svayaṁ ca tattvaṁ svayam-eva buddham.

The six-limbed yoga will not purify you.
Controlling your mind will not purify you.
Listening to a guru's instructions will not purify you.
You are Truth, you are Awareness.

1.49

न हि पञ्चात्मको देहो विदेहो वर्तते न हि ।
आत्मैव केवलं सर्वं तुरीयं च त्रयं कथम् ॥

na hi pañcātmako deho videho vartate na hi,
ātmaiva kevalaṁ sarvaṁ turīyaṁ ca trayaṁ katham.

The Self is neither Embodied in the five elements,
Nor is It Disembodied.
The Self Alone is All.
Where then is the fourth state of mind,
And the other three?

1.50

न बद्धो नैव मुक्तोऽहं न चाहं ब्रह्मणः पृथक् ।
न कर्ता न च भोक्ताहं व्याप्यव्यापकवर्जितः ॥

na baddho naiva mukto'haṁ na cāhaṁ brahmaṇaḥ pṛthak,
na kartā na ca bhoktāhaṁ vyāpya-vyāpaka-varjitaḥ.

I am neither Bound nor Liberated,
Nor am I apart from Brahman.
I am neither Doer nor Enjoyer,
Beyond Pervader and Pervaded.

1.51

यथा जलं जले न्यस्तं सलिलं भेदवर्जितम् ।
प्रकृतिं पुरुषं तद्वदभिन्नं प्रतिभाति मे ॥

yathā jalaṁ jale nyastaṁ salilaṁ bhedavarjitam,
prakṛtiṁ puruṣaṁ tadvad-abhinnaṁ pratibhāti me.

Just as water mixed with water is one water,
With no difference nor demarcation,
So also, I see No Distinction nor Division
Between Puruṣa and Prakriti.

1.52

यदि नाम न मुक्तोऽसि न बद्धोऽसि कदाचन ।
साकारं च निराकारमात्मानं मन्यसे कथम् ॥

yadi nāma na mukto'si na baddho'si kadācana,
sākāraṁ ca nirākāram-ātmānaṁ manyase katham.

If you are not Free,
Nor are you ever Bound.
How then can you think of yourself
As With Form or Without Form?

1.53

जानामि ते परं रूपं प्रत्यक्षं गगनोपमम् ।
यथा परं हि रूपं यन्मरीचिजलसन्निभम् ॥

jānāmi te paraṁ rūpaṁ pratyakṣaṁ gaganopamam,
yathā paraṁ hi rūpaṁ yan-marīci-jala-sannibham.

I know the Supreme One
To be Directly Known like the Sky.
And the same Supreme One
Appears as Forms, like the Waters in a Mirage.

1.54

न गुरुर्नोपदेशश्च न चोपाधिर्न मे क्रिया ।
विदेहं गगनं विद्धि विशुद्धोऽहं स्वभावतः ॥

na guruḥ-nopadeśaś-ca na copādhir-na me kriyā,
videhaṁ gaganaṁ viddhi viśuddho'haṁ svabhāvataḥ.

I have neither Teacher nor Instruction,
Neither Title nor Duty.
Know that I am Formless like the Sky,
And Pure by my Nature.

1.55

विशुद्धोऽस्य शरीरोऽसि न ते चित्तं परात्परम् ।
अहं चात्मा परं तत्त्वमिति वक्तुं न लज्जसे ॥

viśuddho'sya śarīro'si na te cittaṁ parātparam,
ahaṁ cātmā paraṁ tattvam-iti vaktuṁ na lajjase.

You are Very Pure, you have no Body.
You are not the Mind, you are the Most Supreme Truth.
“I am the Self, the Supreme Truth!”
Say this without shyness.

1.56

कथं रोदिषि रे चित्त ह्यात्मैवात्मात्मना भव ।
पिब वत्स कलातीतमद्वैतं परमामृतम् ॥

kathaṁ rodiṣi re citta hy-ātmaivātmātmanā bhava,
piba vatsa kalātītam-advaitaṁ paramāmṛtam.

Why do you weep, O Mind?
You decide, "I am the Self."
O Child, drink the Supreme Nectar of Non-Duality
Which Outshines All!

1.57

नैव बोधो न चाबोधो न बोधाबोध एव च ।
यस्येदृशः सदा बोधः स बोधो नान्यथा भवेत् ॥

naiva bodho na cābodho na bodhābodha eva ca,
yasyedṛśaḥ sadā bodhaḥ sa bodho nānyathā bhavet.

You are neither Knowledge nor Ignorance,
Nor both Knowledge and Ignorance.
He who has this Insight
Becomes Knowledge, and Nothing Else!

1.58

ज्ञानं न तर्को न समाधियोगो न देशकालौ न गुरूपदेशः ।
स्वभावसंवित्तरहं च तत्त्वमाकाशकल्पं सहजं ध्रुवं च ॥

jñānaṁ na tarko na samādhi-yogo
na deśa-kālau na gurūpadeśaḥ,
svabhāva-saṁvittar-ahaṁ ca tattvam-
ākāśa-kalpaṁ sahajaṁ dhruvaṁ ca.

Self-knowledge is not obtained by Reasoning,
Meditation, Guru's Instructions,
Or Things in Space and Time.
I am Naturally Pure Consciousness, the Truth,
Inherently Constant like Space.

1.59

न जातोऽहं मृतो वापि न मे कर्म शुभाशुभम् ।
विशुद्धं निर्गुणं ब्रह्म बन्धो मुक्तिः कथं मम ॥

na jāto'haṁ mṛto vāpi na me karma śubhāśubham,
viśuddhaṁ nirguṇaṁ brahma bandho muktiḥ kathaṁ mama.

I have neither birth nor death,
Nor karma, good nor bad.
I am Brahman, Pure and Free of Qualities.
How can Bondage or Liberation relate to me?

1.60

यदि सर्वगतो देवः स्थिरः पूर्णो निरन्तरः ।
अन्तरं हि न पश्यामि स बाह्याभ्यन्तरः कथम् ॥

yadi sarvagato devaḥ sthiraḥ pūrṇo nirantaraḥ,
antaraṁ hi na paśyāmi sa bāhyābhyantaraḥ katham.

If Brahman is Omnipresent, Luminous,
Immovable, Complete, Constant and Eternal,
Then I see No Division.
How then can It be Inside or Outside?

1.61

स्फुरत्येव जगत्कृत्स्नमखण्डितनिरन्तरम् ।
अहो मायामहामोहो द्वैताद्वैतविकल्पना ॥

sphuratyeva jagat-kṛtsnam-akhaṇḍita-nirantaram,
aho māyā-mahā-moho dvaitādvaita-vikalpanā.

The Whole Universe Shines
As an Undivided Continuum.
O Maya the great delusion,
Has created the dilemma of Duality and Non-Duality.

1.62

साकारं च निराकारं नेति नेतीति सर्वदा ।
भेदाभेदविनिर्मुक्तो वर्तते केवलः शिवः ॥

sākāraṁ ca nirākāraṁ neti netīti sarvadā,
bhedābheda-vinirmukto vartate kevalaḥ śivaḥ.

Form and Formlessness
Have no true Existence.
Free of Duality and Non-Duality,
Śiva Alone Exists!

1.63

न ते च माता च पिता च बन्धुः
न ते च पत्नी न सुतश्च मित्रम् ।
न पक्षपातो न विपक्षपातः
कथं हि संतप्तिरियं हि चित्ते ॥

na te ca mātā ca pitā ca bandhuḥ
na te ca patnī na sutaś-ca mitram,
na pakṣapāto na vipakṣapātaḥ
kathaṁ hi saṁtaptir-iyaṁ hi cite.

You have neither mother nor father,
Relative, wife, son, nor friend.
Nor do you have any Inclinations or Disinclinations.
Why then do you have sorrow in your mind?

1.64

दिवा नक्तं न ते चित्तं उदयास्तमयौ न हि ।
विदेहस्य शरीरत्वं कल्पयन्ति कथं बुधाः ॥

divā naktaṁ na te cittaṁ udayāstamayau na hi,
videhasya śarīratvaṁ kalpayanti kathaṁ budhāḥ.

O Mind, there is neither Day nor Night,
Rising (manifestation), nor Setting (dissolution).
How could the Wise man imagine the formless
As having a body?

1.65

नाविभक्तं विभक्तं च न हि दुःखसुखादि च ।
न हि सर्वमसर्वं च विद्धि चात्मानमव्ययम् ॥

nāvibhaktaṁ vibhaktaṁ ca na hi duḥkha-sukhādi ca,
na hi sarvam-asarvaṁ ca viddhi cātmānam-avyayam.

Neither Undivided nor Divided,
Beyond Joy, Sorrow, and other feelings,
It is neither Everything nor Not Everything.
Know thus the Unchanging Self.

1.66

नाहं कर्ता न भोक्ता च न मे कर्म पुराऽधुना ।
न मे देहो विदेहो वा निर्ममेति ममेति किम् ॥

nāhaṁ kartā na bhoktā ca na me karma purā'dhunā,
na me deho videho vā nirmameti mameti kim.

I am neither Doer nor Enjoyer.
I have no karma, neither present nor past.
I have no body, nor am I bodiless.
What does the sense of my-ness or its absence, mean to me?

1.67

न मे रागादिको दोषो दुःखं देहादिकं न मे ।
आत्मानं विद्धि मामेकं विशालं गगनोपमम् ॥

na me rāgādiko doṣo duḥkhaṁ dehādikaṁ na me,
ātmānaṁ viddhi māmekaṁ viśālaṁ gaganopamam.

Free of attachment and other weaknesses,
Free of pain from the body, and elsewhere,
Know Me to be the One Self,
Vast like the Sky.

1.68

सखे मनः किं बहुजल्पितेन
सखे मनः सर्वमिदं वितर्क्यम् ।
यत्सारभूतं कथितं मया ते
त्वमेव तत्त्वं गगनोपमोऽसि ॥

sakhe manaḥ kiṁ bahu-jalpitena
sakhe manaḥ sarvam-idaṁ vitarkyam,
yat-sāra-bhūtaṁ kathitaṁ mayā te
tvameva tattvaṁ gaganopamo'si.

O Mind, Friend, what good is so much rambling?
O Mind, Friend, all this here is questionable.
I have told you the Essence:
You Yourself are the Truth, Endless like the Sky.

1.69

येन केनापि भावेन यत्र कुत्र मृता अपि ।
योगिनस्तत्र लीयन्ते घटाकाशमिवाम्बरे ॥

yena kenāpi bhāvena yatra kutra mṛtā api,
yoginaḥ-tatra līyante ghaṭākāśam-ivāmbare.

Wherever a yogi dies, in whatever state,
He merges with Truth.
Just like jar space merges with Infinite Space
When the jar is broken.

1.70

तीर्थे चान्त्यजगेहे वा नष्टस्मृतिरपि त्यजन् ।
समकाले तनुं मुक्तः कैवल्यव्यापको भवेत् ॥

tīrthe cāntya-jagehe vā naṣṭa-smṛtir-api tyajan,
samakāle tanuṁ muktaḥ kaivalya-vyāpako bhavet.

A yogi may die in a holy place
Or in the home of an outcaste,
Or he may be unconscious at the time of death,
But as soon as he gives up the body
He attains Freedom, Merging with the One Truth.

1.71

धर्मार्थकाममोक्षांश्च द्विपदादिचराचरम् ।
मन्यन्ते योगिनः सर्वं मरीचिजलसन्निभम् ॥

dharmārtha-kāma-mokṣāṁśca dvipadādi-carācaram,
manyante yoginaḥ sarvaṁ marīci-jala-sannibham.

Duty, wealth, desire, liberation,
Men, movable and immovable objects,
Are all considered by the yogi to be Illusory,
Like the Waters in a Mirage.

1.72

अतीतानागतं कर्म वर्तमानं तथैव च ।
न करोमि न भुञ्जामि इति मे निश्चला मतिः ॥

atītānāgataṁ karma vartamānaṁ tathaiva ca,
na karomi na bhuñjāmi iti me niścalā matiḥ.

I have neither Performed Action
Nor Enjoyed their Fruits,
In the Past, Present, or Future.
This is my Firm Conviction.

1.73

शून्यागारे समरसपूत-
स्तिष्ठन्नेकः सुखमवधूतः ।
चरति हि नग्नस्त्यक्त्वा गर्वं
विन्दति केवलमात्मनि सर्वम् ॥

śūnyāgāre samarasa-pūtaḥ
tiṣṭhan-nekaḥ sukham-avadhūtaḥ,
carati hi nagnaḥ-tyaktvā garvaṁ
vindati kevalam-ātmani sarvam.

The Avadhūta, Pure and Equanimous,
Lives happily alone in a deserted place.
Having renounced all pride, he roams disrobed.
He knows Everything is the Self Alone!

1.74

त्रितयतुरीयं नहि नहि यत्र
विन्दति केवलमात्मनि तत्र ।
धर्माधर्मौ नहि नहि यत्र
बद्धो मुक्तः कथमिह तत्र ॥

tritaya-turīyaṁ nahi nahi yatra
vindati kevalam-ātmani tatra,
dharmādharmau nahi nahi yatra
baddho muktaḥ katham-iha tatra.

Where there are not the three states, nor the fourth,
There the Self Alone is attained.
Where there is neither Virtue nor Vice,
How can there be Bondage or Freedom?

1.75

विन्दति विन्दति नहि नहि मन्त्रं
छन्दोलक्षणं नहि नहि तन्त्रम् ।
समरसमग्नो भावितपूतः
प्रलपितमेतत्परमवधूतः ॥

vindati vindati nahi nahi mantraṁ
chando-lakṣaṇaṁ nahi nahi tantram,
samarasa-magno bhāvita-pūtaḥ
pralapitam-etat-param-avadhūtaḥ.

The Avadhūta does not know mantras, verses, or tantra.
Purified by Meditation,
Deeply absorbed in Absolute Equanimity,
The Avadhūta has spoken the Supreme Truth.

1.76

सर्वशून्यमशून्यं च सत्यासत्यं न विद्यते ।
स्वभावभावतः प्रोक्तं शास्त्रसंवित्तिपूर्वकम् ॥

sarva-śūnyam-aśūnyaṁ ca satyāsatyaṁ na vidyate,
svabhāva-bhāvataḥ proktaṁ śāstra-saṁvitti-pūrvakam.

Everything is Empty and Full.
There is neither Truth nor Untruth.
The Avadhūta declares this from his Wisdom,
And all the Scriptures affirm it.

Chapter 2

The Perfect One Is The Lord of the Universe!

2.1

बालस्य वा विषयभोगरतस्य वापि
मूर्खस्य सेवकजनस्य गृहस्थितस्य ।
एतद्गुरोः किमपि नैव न चिन्तनीयं
रत्नं कथं त्यजति कोऽप्यशुचौ प्रविष्टम् ॥

bālasya vā viṣaya-bhoga-ratasya vāpi
mūrkhasya sevaka-janasya gṛha-sthitasya,
etad-guroḥ kim-api naiva na cintanīyaṁ
ratnaṁ kathaṁ tyajati ko'pyaśucau praviṣṭam.

Even if a teacher is young,
Pleasure-seeking, unlettered, attendant, or householder,
He should not be discounted.
Does one disown a gem fallen in dirt?

2.2

नैवात्र काव्यगुण एव तु चिन्तनीयो
ग्राह्यः परं गुणवता खलु सार एव ।
सिन्दूरचित्ररहिता भुवि रूपशून्या
पारं न किं नयति नौरिह गन्तुकामान् ॥

naivātra kāvya-guṇa eva tu cintanīyo
grāhyaḥ paraṁ guṇavatā khalu sāra eva,
sindūra-citra-rahitā bhuvi rūpa-śūnyā
pāraṁ na kiṁ nayati naur-iha gantu-kāmān.

Do not judge a guru by his degree of learnedness,
Instead, grasp the Essence of his teaching.
Does not a plain, unpainted boat
Carry people across?

2.3

प्रयत्नेन विना येन निश्चलेन चलाचलम् ।
ग्रस्तं स्वभावतः शान्तं चैतन्यं गगनोपमम् ॥

prayatnena vinā yena niścalena calācalam,
grastaṁ svabhāvataḥ śāntaṁ caitanyaṁ gaganopamam.

Effortlessly, the Motionless Self appears
As both Moving and Unmoving Objects.
Absorbed in Itself, Peaceful by Its Nature,
It is Consciousness, Pervasive like the Sky.

2.4

अयत्नाच्चालयेद्यस्तु एकमेव चराचरम् ।
सर्वगं तत्कथं भिन्नमद्वैतं वर्तते मम ॥

ayatnāc-cālayed-yastu ekam-eva carācaram,
sarvagaṁ tat-kathaṁ bhinnam-advaitaṁ vartate mama.

Effortlessly, It guides
Both Moving and Unmoving Objects.
How can that All-Pervasive One
Be other than Me?

2.5

अहमेव परं यस्मात्सारात्साररतरं शिवम् ।
गमागमविनिर्मुक्तं निर्विकल्पं निराकुलम् ॥

aham-eva paraṁ yasmāt-sārāt-sārataraṁ śivam,
gamāgama-vinirmuktaṁ nirvikalpaṁ nirākulam.

I am the Supreme,
The Essence of all Essences, I am Śiva,
Free of birth and death,
Qualm and confusion.

2.6

सर्वावयवनिर्मुक्तं तथाहं त्रिदशार्चितम् ।
सम्पूर्णत्वान्न गृह्णामि विभागं त्रिदशादिकम् ॥

sarvāvaya-vanirmuktaṁ tathāhaṁ tridaśā-arcitam,
sampūrṇatvān-na gṛhṇāmi vibhāgaṁ tridaśādikam.

Impartible and worshipped by Gods,
Full and Perfect,
I do not distinguish differences such as Gods,
Within my Wholeness.

2.7

प्रमादेन न सन्देहः किं करिष्यामि वृत्तिमान् ।
उत्पद्यन्ते विलीयन्ते बुद्बुदाश्च यथा जले ॥

pramādena na sandehaḥ kiṁ kariṣyāmi vṛttimān,
utpadyante vilīyante budbudāś-ca yathā jale.

Ignorance does not create qualm in me.
The modifications of the mind
Are like bubbles,
Rising and disappearing in water.

2.8

महदादीनि भूतानि समाप्यैवं सदैव हि ।
मृदुद्रव्येषु तीक्ष्णेषु गुडेषु कटुकेषु च ॥

mahadādīni bhūtāni samāpyaivaṁ sadaiva hi,
mṛdudravyeṣu tīkṣṇeṣu guḍeṣu kaṭukeṣu ca.

I pervade all Existence
As well as Cosmic Intelligence,
Just as softness, hardness, sweetness, and bitterness
Inseparably pervade their respective substances.

2.9

कटुत्वं चैव शैत्यत्वं मृदुत्वं च यथा जले ।
प्रकृतिः पुरुषस्तद्वदभिन्नं प्रतिभाति मे ॥

kaṭutvaṁ caiva śaityatvaṁ mṛdutvaṁ ca yathā jale,
prakṛtiḥ puruṣaḥ-tadvat-abhinnaṁ pratibhāti me.

Just as bitterness, coldness, and softness
Are inseparably and indistinguishably one with water,
So also, Prakriti and Puruṣa
Are Inextricably and Completely One,
And Cannot Be Separated from Each Other.

2.10

सर्वाख्यारहितं यद्यत्सूक्ष्मात्सूक्ष्मतरं परम् ।
मनोबुद्धीन्द्रियातीतमकलङ्कं जगत्पतिम् ॥

sarvākhyā-rahitaṁ yad-yat-sūkṣmat-sūkṣmataraṁ param,
manobuddhī-indriyātītam-akalaṅkaṁ jagatpatim.

Free of Names, the Subtlest of the Subtle,
Beyond the Mind, Intellect, and Senses,
The Perfect One
Is The Lord of the Universe!

2.11

ईदृशं सहजं यत्र अहं तत्र कथं भवेत् ।
त्वमेव हि कथं तत्र कथं तत्र चराचरम् ॥

īdṛśaṁ sahajaṁ yatra ahaṁ tatra kathaṁ bhavet,
tvameva hi kathaṁ tatra kathaṁ tatra carācaram.

If such is the Original Being,
How can there be an I?
Or a You?
Or a World of Movable and Immovable Objects?

2.12

गगनोपमं तु यत्प्रोक्तं तदेव गगनोपमम् ।
चैतन्यं दोषहीनं च सर्वज्ञं पूर्णमेव च ॥

gaganopamaṁ tu yat-proktaṁ tad-eva gaganopamam,
caitanyaṁ doṣa-hīnaṁ ca sarvajñaṁ pūrṇam-eva ca.

It has been described as Space,
And like Space It is All-Pervasive.
It is Consciousness,
Flawless, Omniscient, and Entire.

2.13

पृथिव्यां चरितं नैव मारुतेन च वाहितम् ।
वरिणा पिहितं नैव तेजोमध्ये व्यवस्थितम् ॥

pṛthivyāṁ caritaṁ naiva mārutena ca vāhitam,
variṇā pihitaṁ naiva tejomadhye vyavasthitam.

It does not move on land,
Nor is It blown by wind,
Or covered by water,
Or bide in fire.

2.14

आकाशं तेन संव्याप्तं न तद्व्याप्तं च केनचित् ।
स बाह्याभ्यन्तरं तिष्ठत्यवच्छिन्नं निरन्तरम् ॥

ākāśaṁ tena saṁvyāptaṁ na tadvyāptaṁ ca kenacit,
sa bāhyābhyantaraṁ tiṣṭhat-yavat-cchinnaṁ nirantaram.

Space is pervaded by It,
But It is not pervaded by anything.
Existing both Within and Without,
It is Undivided, Uninterrupted, and Unending.

2.15

सूक्ष्मत्वात्तदद्दश्यत्वान्निर्गुणत्वाच्च योगिभिः ।
आलम्बनादि यत्प्रोक्तं क्रमादालम्बनं भवेत् ॥

sūkṣmatvāt-tad-adṛśyatvāt-nirguṇatvāc-ca yogibhiḥ,
ālaṁbanādi yat-proktaṁ kramād-ālaṁbanaṁ bhavet.

It is Subtle,
Beyond Perception and Attributes,
Say the yogis.
The practices for realization should be followed serially.

2.16

सतताऽभ्यासयुक्तस्तु निरालम्बो यदा भवेत् ।
तल्लयाल्लीयते नान्तर्गुणदोषविवर्जितः ॥

satatā'bhyāsa-yuktas-tu nirālaṁbo yadā bhavet,
tal-layāt-līyate nāntar-guṇadoṣa-vivarjitaḥ.

Through constant practice
The mind becomes Objectless,
And attains Dissolution in the Absolute,
Going beyond good and evil.

2.17

विषविश्वस्य रौद्रस्य मोहमूर्च्छाप्रदस्य च ।
एकमेव विनाशाय ह्यमोघं सहजामृतम् ॥

viṣa-viśvasya raudrasya moha-mūrcchā-pradasya ca,
ekam-eva vināśāya hyamoghaṁ sahajāmṛtam.

The poison of Infatuation with the World,
That causes the Trance of Delusion
Can only be overcome
By the Nectar of Truth.

2.18

भावगम्यं निराकारं साकारं दृष्टिगोचरम् ।
भावाभावविनिर्मुक्तमन्तरालं तदुच्यते ॥

bhāva-gamyaṁ nirākāraṁ sākāraṁ drṣṭi-gocharam,
bhāvābhāva-vinirmuktam-antarālaṁ tad-ucyate.

The Formless is seen in the Mind,
While Form is seen with the Eyes.
Beyond both the Manifest and the Unmanifest,
Is the Inner Self.

2.19

बाह्यभावं भवेद्विश्वमन्तः प्रकृतिरुच्यते ।
अन्तरादन्तरं ज्ञेयं नारिकेलफलाम्बुवत् ॥

bāhya-bhāvaṁ bhaved-viśvam-antaḥ prakṛtir-ucyate,
antarādantaraṁ jñeyaṁ nārikela-phalāmbuvat.

The external manifestation is the Universe.
Its hidden cause is Prakriti or Maya.
The hidden cause of Prakriti is Brahman.
Realize Brahman which is the Innermost of the Inner Self –
The Water within the Coconut.

2.20

भ्रान्तिज्ञानं स्थितं बाह्यं सम्यग्ज्ञानं च मध्यगम् ।
मध्यान्मध्यतरं ज्ञेयं नारिकेलफलाम्बुवत् ॥

bhrānti-jñānaṁ sthitaṁ bāhyaṁ samyag-jñānaṁ ca madhyagam,
madhyān-madhyataraṁ jñeyaṁ nārikela-phalāmbuvat.

False Knowledge relates to the Outer World.
True Knowledge relates to what is Inside.
Realize Brahman which is the Innermost of the Inner Self –
The Water within the Coconut.

2.21

पौर्णमास्यां यथा चन्द्र एक एवातिनिर्मलः ।
तेन तत्सदृशं पश्येद्द्विधादृष्टिर्विपर्ययः ॥

paurṇamāsyāṁ yathā candra eka evātinirmalaḥ,
tena tat-sadṛśaṁ paśyet-dvidhā-dṛṣṭih-viparyayaḥ.

Just as the Moon is seen
As One and Bright on a Full Moon Night,
So also Brahman should be seen as One and Effulgent.
Duality is the result of Imperfect Vision.

2.22

अनेनैव प्रकारेण बुद्धिभेदो न सर्वगः ।
दाता च धीरतामेति गीयते नामकोटिभिः ॥

anenaiva prakāreṇa buddhi-bhedo na sarvagaḥ,
dātā ca dhīratām-eti gīyate nāma-koṭibhiḥ.

In this manner (because of imperfect vision),
A mind that is divided
Is unable to see the Whole.
The Purified One attains Wisdom,
And is praised a million times.

2.23

गुरुप्रज्ञाप्रसादेन मूर्खो वा यदि पण्डितः ।
यस्तु सम्बुध्यते तत्त्वं विरक्तो भवसागरात् ॥

guru-prajñā-prasādena mūrkho vā yadi paṇḍitaḥ,
yastu sambudhyate tattvaṁ virakto bhava-sāgarāt.

A guru gives Wisdom
To the learned and the unlearned.
Only he who realizes the Truth
Crosses the Ocean of Maya.

2.24

रागद्वेषविनिर्मुक्तः सर्वभूतहिते रतः ।
दृढबोधश्च धीरश्च स गच्छेत्परमं पदम् ॥

rāgadveṣa-vinirmuktaḥ sarvabhūta-hite rataḥ,
dṛḍha-bodhas-ca dhīras-ca sa gacchet-paramaṁ padam.

Free of Attachment and Aversion,
Devoted to the Well-being of All,
Poised and Firm in Knowledge,
The Wise One attains the Supreme State.

2.25

घटे भिन्ने घटाकाश आकाशे लीयते यथा ।
देहाभावे तथा योगी स्वरूपे परमात्मनि ॥

ghaṭe bhinne ghaṭākāśa ākāśe līyate yathā,
dehābhāve tathā yogī swarūpe paramātmani.

Just like jar space merges with Infinite Space
When the jar is broken,
So also, when a yogi dies
He melds into his True Nature, the Supreme Self.

2.26

उक्तेयं कर्मयुक्तानां मतिर्यान्तेऽपि सा गतिः ।
न चोक्ता योगयुक्तानां मतिर्यान्तेऽपि सा गतिः ॥

ukteyaṁ karma-yuktānāṁ matir-yānte'pi sā gatiḥ,
na coktā yoga-yuktānāṁ matir-yānte'pi sā gatiḥ.

It has been said,
The destiny of those devoted to Action
Is determined by their thoughts at the time of death.
This has not been stated for the devotees of Yoga.

2.27

या गतिः कर्मयुक्तानां सा च वागिन्द्रियाद्वदेत् ।
योगिनां या गतिः क्वापि ह्यकथ्या भवतोर्जिता ॥

yā gatiḥ karmayuktānāṁ sā ca vāgindriyādvadet,
yogināṁ yā gatiḥ kvāpi hy-akathyā bhavatorjitā.

The destiny of one devoted to Action
Can be described by speech.
But the destiny of the Yogi cannot be described.
It is beyond speech.

2.28

एवं ज्ञात्वा त्वमुं मार्गं योगिनां नैव कल्पितम् ।
विकल्पवर्जनं तेषां स्वयं सिद्धिः प्रवर्तते ॥

evaṁ jñātvā twamuṁ mārgaṁ yogināṁ naiva kalpitam,
vikalpa-varjanaṁ teṣāṁ swayaṁ siddhiḥ pravartate.

Knowing this, one does not suppose
A particular path for the yogi.
Having Relinquished Duality,
Self-realization is Natural for him.

2.29

तीर्थे वान्त्यजगेहे वा यत्र कुत्र मृतोऽपि वा ।
न योगी पश्यते गर्भं परे ब्रह्मणि लीयते ॥

tirthe vā-antyaja-gehe vā yatra kutra mṛto'pi vā,
na yogī paśyate garbhaṁ pare brahmaṇi līyate.

A yogi may die in a holy place
Or in an outcaste's place,
But he never again enters into a mother's womb.
He becomes One in Brahman.

2.30

सहजमजमचिन्त्यं यस्तु पश्येत्स्वरूपं
घटति यदि यथेष्टं लिप्यते नैव दोषैः ।
सकृदपि तदभावात्कर्म किंचिन्नकुर्यात्
तदपि न च विबद्धः संयमी वा तपस्वी ॥

sahajam-ajam-acintyaṁ yastu paśyet-swarūpaṁ
ghaṭati yadi yatheṣṭaṁ lipyate naiva doṣaiḥ,
sakṛd-api tadabhāvāt-karma kiñchin-na-kuryāt
tad-api na ca vibaddaḥ saṁyamī vā tapasvī.

One who has known
His Essential Unborn Incomprehensible Self,
Is never tainted by any Action.
Free of Ignorance, he is Free of Action.
The Ascetic, fixated on the Self, is never bound.

2.31

निरामयं निष्प्रतिमं निराकृतिं
निराश्रयं निर्वपुषं निराशिषम् ।
निर्द्वन्द्वनिर्मोहमलुप्तशक्तिकं
तमीशमात्मानमुपैति शाश्वतम् ॥

nirāmayaṁ niṣpratimaṁ nirākṛtiṁ
nirāśrayaṁ nirvāpuṣaṁ nirāśiṣam,
nirdvandva-nirmoham-alupta-śaktikaṁ
tam-īśam-ātmānam-upaiti śāśvatam.

He attains The Lord, the Self, the Eternal -
Pure, Incomparable, Formless,
Transcending support, body, desire,
The pairs of opposites and illusion,
And of Undiminished Power.

2.32

वेदो न दीक्षा न च मुण्डनक्रिया
गुरुर्न शिष्यो न च यन्त्रसम्पदः ।
मुद्रादिकं चापि न यत्र भासते
तमीशमात्मानमुपैति शाश्वतम् ॥

vedo na dīkṣā na ca muṇḍana-kriyā
gurur-na śiṣyo na ca yantra-sampadaḥ,
mudrādikaṁ cāpi na yatra bhāsate
tam-īśam-ātmānam-upaiti śāśvatam.

The yogi attains The Lord, the Self, the Eternal -
Not the Vedas, initiation or shaven head,
Nor guru nor discipleship,
Nor possessions nor wealth,
Nor symbolic figures nor hand postures.

2.33

न शाम्भवं शाक्तिकमानवं न वा
पिण्डं च रूपं च पदादिकं न वा ।
आरम्भनिष्पत्तिघटादिकं च नो
तमीशमात्मानमुपैति शाश्वतम् ॥

na śāmbhavaṁ śāktika-mānavaṁ na vā
piṇḍaṁ ca rūpaṁ ca padādikaṁ na vā,
ārambha-niṣpatti-ghaṭādikaṁ ca no
tam-īśam-ātmānam-upaiti śāśvatam.

The yogi attains The Lord, the Self, the Eternal –
Not Śiva or Śakti or human,
Not the body, the form, or the feet of the Lord,
Not the beginning, the middle, or the end.

2.34

यस्य स्वरूपात्सचराचरं जगद्
उत्पद्यते तिष्ठति लीयतेऽपि वा ।
पयोविकारादिव फेनबुद्बुदा-
स्तमीशमात्मानमुपैति शाश्वतम् ॥

yasya svarūpāt-sacarācaraṁ jagad
utpadyate tiṣṭhati līyate'pi vā,
payo-vikārād-iva phena-budbudās-
tam-īśam-ātmānam-upaiti śāśvatam.

The yogi attains The Lord, the Self, the Eternal –
The Essence from which the Sentient and Insentient World
Is born, maintained, and merges into,
Like foam and bubbles arising and disappearing in the
ocean.

2.35

नासानिरोधो न च दृष्टिरासनं
बोधोऽप्यबोधोऽपि न यत्र भासते।
नाडीप्रचारोऽपि न यत्र किञ्चित्-
तमीशमात्मानमुपैति शाश्वतम् ॥

nāsā-nirodho na ca dṛṣṭir-āsanaṁ
bodho'pyabodho'pi na yatra bhāsate,
nāḍi-pracāro'pi na yatra kiñchit
tam-īśam-ātmānam-upaiti śāśvatam.

The yogi attains The Lord, the Self, the Eternal –
Not breath-control, nor gazing, nor posture,
Neither knowledge nor ignorance,
Nor the purification of nerves.

2.36

नानात्वमेकत्वमुभत्वमन्यता
अणुत्वदीर्घत्वमहत्त्वशून्यता ।
मानत्वमेयत्वसमत्ववर्जितं
तमीशमात्मानमुपैति शाश्वतम् ॥

nānātvam-ekatvam-ubhatvam-anyatā
aṇutva-dīrghatva-mahatva-śūnyatā,
mānatva-meyatva-samatva-varjitaṁ
tam-īśam-ātmānam-upaiti śāśvatam.

The yogi attains The Lord, the Self, the Eternal –
Not the Many nor the One, nor both, nor another.
Devoid of minuteness, magnitude, enormity, and emptiness,
Beyond contrast and comparison.

2.37

सुसंयमी वा यदि वा न संयमी
सुसंग्रही वा यदि वा न संग्रही ।
निष्कर्मको वा यदि वा सकर्मक-
स्तमीशमात्मानमुपैति शाश्वतम् ॥

susaṁyamī vā yadi vā na saṁyamī
susangrahī vā yadi vā na sangrahī,
niṣkarmako vā yadi vā sakarmakaḥ
tam-īśam-ātmānam-upaiti śāśvatam.

The yogi attains The Lord, the Self, the Eternal –
Whether he is Disciplined or Undisciplined,
Worldly or Unworldly,
Active or Inactive.

2.38

मनो न बुद्धिर्न शरीरमिन्द्रियं
तन्मात्रभूतानि न भूतपञ्चकम् ।
अहंकृतिश्चापि वियत्स्वरूपकं
तमीशमात्मानमुपैति शाश्वतम् ॥

mano na buddhiḥ-na śarīram-indriyaṁ
tanmātra-bhūtāni na bhūta-pañcakam,
ahaṁkṛtiś-cāpi viyat-swarūpakaṁ
tam-īśam-ātmānam-upaiti śāśvatam.

The yogi attains The Lord, the Self, the Eternal –
Beyond mind, intellect, body, and senses,
Beyond the subtle elements, the five gross elements, and the ego,
Of the nature of Space.

2.39

विधौ निरोधे परमात्मतां गते
न योगिनश्चेतसि भेदवर्जिते ।
शौचं न वाशौचमलिङ्गभावना
सर्वं विधेयं यदि वा निषिध्यते ॥

vidhau nirodhe paramātmatāṁ gate
na yoginaś-cetasi bhedavarjite,
śaucaṁ na vāśaucam-aliṅgabhāvanā
sarvaṁ vidheyaṁ yadi vā niṣidhyate.

When he attains the Supreme Self,
Precepts no longer apply to him.
Free of Duality, he is beyond Purity and Impurity.
No evil thought arises in his mind.
What is forbidden to others is permissible to him.

2.40

मनो वचो यत्र न शक्तमीरितुं
नूनं कथं तत्र गुरूपदेशता ।
इमां कथामुक्तवतो गुरोस्त-
द्युक्तस्य तत्त्वं हि समं प्रकाशते ॥

mano vaco yatra na śaktam-īrituṁ
nūnaṁ kathaṁ tatra gurūpadeśatā,
imāṁ kathām-uktavato guroḥ-tad
yuktasya tattvaṁ hi samaṁ prakāśate.

If the Mind and Speech cannot reveal the Self,
Then how can the Words of the Guru?
The Guru who speaks these Words
Is One with the Self and sees the Truth.

Chapter 3

The Whole is Eternal and Non-Eternal

3.1

गुणविगुणविभागो वर्तते नैव किञ्चित्
रतिविरतिविहीनं निर्मलं निष्प्रपञ्चम् ।
गुणविगुणविहीनं व्यापकं विश्वरूपं
कथमहमिह वन्दे व्योमरूपं शिवं वै ॥

guṇa-viguṇa-vibhāgo vartate naiva kiñcit
rati-virati-vihīnaṁ nirmalaṁ niṣprapañcam,
guṇa-viguṇa-vihīnaṁ vyāpakaṁ viśva-rūpaṁ
katham-aham-iha vande vyoma-rūpaṁ śivaṁ vai.

Beyond Attributes and No Attributes,
Beyond Attachment and No Attachment,
Unblemished, Unfettered by Maya,
Free of Merit and Demerit, Suffused in the Universe,
How shall I worship this Śiva
Who is formless like Space?

3.2

श्वेतादिवर्णरहितो नियतं शिवश्च
कार्यं हि कारणमिदं हि परं शिवश्च ।
एवं विकल्परहितोऽहमलं शिवश्च
स्वात्मानमात्मनि सुमित्र कथं नमामि ॥

śvetādi-varṇa-rahito niyataṁ śivaś-ca
kāryaṁ hi kāraṇam-idam hi paraṁ śivaś-ca,
evaṁ vikalparahito'ham-alaṁ śivaś-ca
swātmānam-ātmani sumitra kathaṁ namāmi.

Ever beyond Colors such as white, He is Eternal.
Beyond both Cause and Effect, He is The Supreme.
Unquestionably, I am the Pure Śiva.
O Dear Friend, how can I, the Self,
Bow down to the Self?

3.3

निर्मूलमूलरहितो हि सदोदितोऽहं
निर्धूमधूमरहितो हि सदोदितोऽहम् ।
निर्दीपदीपरहितो हि सदोदितोऽहं
ज्ञानामृतं समरसं गगनोपमोऽहम् ॥

nirmūla-mūla-rahito hi sadodito'haṁ
nirdhūma-dhūma-rahito hi sadodito'ham,
nirdīpa-dīpa-rahito hi sadodito'haṁ
jñānāmṛtaṁ samarasaṁ gaganopamo'ham.

Beyond Uncreated and Created,
Ever Existing am I.
Beyond Ambiguity and Clarity,
Ever Existing am I.
Beyond Darkness and Light,
Ever Existing am I.
Essence of Wisdom, Serene Blissfulness,
Infinite as Space am I.

3.4

निष्कामकाममिह नाम कथं वदामि
निःसङ्गसङ्गमिह नाम कथं वदामि ।
निःसारसाररहितं च कथं वदामि
ज्ञानामृतं समरसं गगनोपमोऽहम् ॥

niṣkāma-kāmam-iha nāma kathaṁ vadāmi
nissaṅga-saṅgam-iha nāma kathaṁ vadāmi,
nissāra-sāra-rahitaṁ ca kathaṁ vadāmi
jñānāmṛtaṁ samarasaṁ gaganopamo'ham.

How can I call the Desireless One Desirous?
How can I call the Unattached One Attached?
How can I call the Immaterial One Material?
Essence of Wisdom, Serene Blissfulness,
Infinite as Space am I.

3.5

अद्वैतरूपमखिलं हि कथं वदामि
द्वैतस्वरूपमखिलं हि कथं वदामि ।
नित्यं त्वनित्यमखिलं हि कथं वदामि
ज्ञानामृतं समरसं गगनोपमोऽहम् ॥

advaita-rūpam-akhilaṁ hi kathaṁ vadāmi
dvaita-swarūpam-akhilaṁ hi kathaṁ vadāmi,
nityaṁ twanityam-akhilaṁ hi kathaṁ vadāmi
jñānāmṛtaṁ samarasaṁ gaganopamo'ham.

The Whole which is Non-dual,
How shall I convey that?
The Whole which is Dual,
How shall I convey that?
The Whole which is Eternal and Non-Eternal,
How shall I convey that?
Essence of Wisdom, Serene Blissfulness,
Infinite as Space am I.

3.6

स्थूलं हि नो नहि कृशं न गतागतं हि
आद्यन्तमध्यरहितं न परापरं हि ।
सत्यं वदामि खलु वै परमार्थतत्त्वं
ज्ञानामृतं समरसं गगनोपमोऽहम् ॥

sthūlaṁ hi no nahi kṛśaṁ na gatāgataṁ hi
ādyanta-madhya-rahitaṁ na parāparaṁ hi,
satyaṁ vadāmi khalu vai paramārtha-tattvaṁ
jñānāmṛtaṁ samarasaṁ gaganopamo'ham.

I am neither Gross nor Subtle,
I neither Come nor Go,
I have neither Beginning, Middle nor End,
I am neither Higher nor Lower,
I Verily Affirm the Ultimate Truth:
Essence of Wisdom, Serene Blissfulness,
Infinite as Space am I.

3.7

संविद्धि सर्वकरणानि नभोनिभानि
संविद्धि सर्वविषयांश्च नभोनिभांश्च ।
संविद्धि चैकममलं न हि बन्धमुक्तं
ज्ञानामृतं समरसं गगनोपमोऽहम् ॥

saṁviddhi sarva-karaṇāni nabho-nibhāni
saṁviddhi sarva-viṣayāṁś-ca nabho-nibhaṁś-ca,
saṁviddhi caikam-amalaṁ na hi bandhamuktaṁ
jñānāmṛtaṁ samarasaṁ gaganopamo'ham.

Know all Sense Organs to be Empty like the Sky.
Know all Sense Objects to be Empty like the Sky.
Know the Only Pure One, neither Bound nor Free.
Essence of Wisdom, Serene Blissfulness,
Infinite as Space am I.

3.8

दुर्बोधबोधगहनो न भवामि तात
दुर्लक्ष्यलक्ष्यगहनो न भवामि तात ।
आसन्नरूपगहनो न भवामि तात
ज्ञानामृतं समरसं गगनोपमोऽहम् ॥

durbodha-bodha-gahano na bhavāmi tāta
durlakṣya-lakṣya-gahano na bhavāmi tāta,
āsanna-rūpa-gahano na bhavāmi tāta
jñānāmṛtaṁ samarasaṁ gaganopamo'ham.

I am neither Difficult to Comprehend,
Nor Impenetrable to the Intellect, My Child.
I am neither Difficult to Perceive,
Nor Impenetrable to Perception, My Child.
I am not Inaccessible in nearby Forms, My Child.
Essence of Wisdom, Serene Blissfulness,
Infinite as Space am I.

3.9

निष्कर्मकर्मदहनो ज्वलनो भवामि
निर्दुःखदुःखदहनो ज्वलनो भवामि ।
निर्देहदेहदहनो ज्वलनो भवामि
ज्ञानामृतं समरसं गगनोपमोऽहम् ॥

niṣkarma-karma-dahano jvalano bhavāmi
nirduḥkha-duḥkha-dahano jvalano bhavāmi,
nirdeha-deha-dahano jvalano bhavāmi
jñānāmṛtaṁ samarasaṁ gaganopamo'ham.

I am the Fire that burns the Actions
Of the One who is Beyond Action.
I am the Fire that burns the Sorrows
Of the One who is Beyond Sorrow.
I am the fire that burns the Body
Of the One who is Beyond Bodies.
Essence of Wisdom, Serene Blissfulness,
Infinite as Space am I.

3.10

निष्पापपापदहनो हि हुताशनोऽहं
निर्धर्मधर्मदहनो हि हुताशनोऽहम् ।
निर्बन्धबन्धदहनो हि हुताशनोऽहं
ज्ञानामृतं समरसं गगनोपमोऽहम् ॥

niṣpāpa-pāpa-dahano hi hutāśano'haṁ
nirdharma-dharma-dahano hi hutāśano'ham,
nirbandha-bandha-dahano hi hutāśano'haṁ
jñānāmṛtaṁ samarasaṁ gaganopamo'ham.

I am the Fire that burns the Sins
Of the One who is Beyond Sin.
I am the Fire that burns the Duties
Of the One who is Beyond Duty.
I am the Fire that burns the Bondage
Of the One who is Beyond Bondage.
Essence of Wisdom, Serene Blissfulness,
Infinite as Space am I.

3.11

निर्भावभावरहितो न भवामि वत्स
निर्योगयोगरहितो न भवामि वत्स ।
निश्चित्तचित्तरहितो न भवामि वत्स
ज्ञानामृतं समरसं गगनोपमोऽहम् ॥

nirbhāva-bhāvarahito na bhavāmi vatsa
niryoga-yoga-rahito na bhavāmi vatsa,
niścitta-citta-rahito na bhavāmi vatsa
jñānāmṛtaṁ samarasaṁ gaganopamo'ham.

Independent of Nonexistence and Existence,
These do not apply to me, My Child.
Independent of Separation and Union,
These do not apply to me, My Child.
Independent of Mindlessness and Mindfulness,
These do not apply to me, My Child.
Essence of Wisdom, Serene Blissfulness,
Infinite as Space am I.

3.12

निर्मोहमोहपदवीति न मे विकल्पो
निःशोकशोकपदवीति न मे विकल्पः ।
निर्लोभलोभपदवीति न मे विकल्पो
ज्ञानामृतं समरसं गगनोपमोऽहम् ॥

nirmoha-moha-padavīti na me vikalpo
niśśoka-śoka-padavīti na me vikalpaḥ,
nirlobha-lobha-padavīti na me vikalpo
jñānāmṛtaṁ samarasaṁ gaganopamo'ham.

The Undeluded appears to be Deluded –
This does not befuddle me.
The Unsorrowful appears to be Sorrowful –
This does not befuddle me.
The Uncovetous appears to be Covetous –
This does not befuddle me.
Essence of Wisdom, Serene Blissfulness,
Infinite as Space am I.

3.13

संसारसन्ततिलता न च मे कदाचित्
सन्तोषसन्ततिसुखो न च मे कदाचित् ।
अज्ञानबन्धनमिदं न च मे कदाचित्
ज्ञानामृतं समरसं गगनोपमोऽहम् ॥

saṁsāra-santati-latā na ca me kadācit
santoṣa-santati-sukho na ca me kadācit,
ajñāna-bandhanam-idaṁ na ca me kadācit
jñānāmṛtaṁ samarasaṁ gaganopamo'ham.

The Creeper of Samsara never dwells in Me.
The Joy of Contentment never dwells in Me.
The Bondage of Ignorance never dwells in Me.
Essence of Wisdom, Serene Blissfulness,
Infinite as Space am I.

3.14

संसारसन्ततिरजो न च मे विकारः
सन्तापसन्ततितमो न च मे विकारः ।
सत्त्वं स्वधर्मजनकं न च मे विकारो
ज्ञानामृतं समरसं गगनोपमोऽहम् ॥

saṁsāra-santati-rajo na ca me vikāraḥ
santāpa-santati-tamo na ca me vikāraḥ,
satvaṁ swadharma-janakaṁ na ca me vikaraḥ
jñānāmṛtaṁ samarasaṁ gaganopamo'ham.

Samsar, a product of rajas, is not a ripple in Me.
Sorrow, a product of tamas, is not a ripple in Me.
Happiness, a product of sattva, is not a ripple in Me.
Essence of Wisdom, Serene Blissfulness,
Infinite as Space am I.

3.15

सन्तापदुःखजनको न विधिः कदाचित्
सन्तापयोगजनितं न मनः कदाचित् ।
यस्मादहङ्कृतिरियं न च मे कदाचित्
ज्ञानामृतं समरसं गगनोपमोऽहम् ॥

santāpa-duḥkha-janako na vidhiḥ kadācit
santāpa-yoga-janitaṁ na manaḥ kadācit,
yasmād-ahankṛtiriyaṁ na ca me kadācit
jñānāmṛtaṁ samarasaṁ gaganopamo'ham.

Actions that lead to sorrow and regret are never in Me.
A Mind afflicted with pain is never in Me.
Because Egoism is never in Me.
Essence of Wisdom, Serene Blissfulness,
Infinite as Space am I.

3.16

निष्कम्पकम्पनिधनं न विकल्पकल्पं
स्वप्नप्रबोधनिधनं न हिताहितं हि ।
निःसारसारनिधनं न चराचरं हि
ज्ञानामृतं समरसं गगनोपमोऽहम् ॥

niṣkampa-kampa-nidhanaṁ na vikalpa-kalpaṁ
svapna-prabodha-nidhanaṁ na hitāhitaṁ hi,
nissāra-sāra-nidhanaṁ na carācaraṁ hi
jñānāmṛtaṁ samarasaṁ gaganopamo'ham.

Having ended both Unwavering and Wavering,
I am beyond Doubt and Determination.
Having ended both Dream and Waking,
I am beyond Good and Evil.
Having ended both Insubstantial and Substantial,
I am beyond Animate and Inanimate.
Essence of Wisdom, Serene Blissfulness,
Infinite as Space am I.

3.17

नो वेद्यवेदकमिदं न च हेतुतर्क्यं
वाचामगोचरमिदं न मनो न बुद्धिः ।
एवं कथं हि भवतः कथयामि तत्त्वं
ज्ञानामृतं समरसं गगनोपमोऽहम् ॥

no vedya-vedakam-idaṁ na ca hetu-tarkyaṁ
vācāmagocaram-idaṁ na mano na buddhiḥ,
evaṁ kathaṁ hi bhavataḥ kathayāmi tattvaṁ
jñānāmṛtaṁ samarasaṁ gaganopamo'ham.

I am neither the Knowable nor the Knowing,
Neither the Reason nor the Reasoned,
Beyond Speech, Mind, and Intellect,
How shall I speak this Ultimate Truth to you?
Essence of Wisdom, Serene Blissfulness,
Infinite as Space am I.

3.18

निर्भिन्नभिन्नरहितं परमार्थतत्त्व-
मन्तर्बहिर्न हि कथं परमार्थतत्त्वम् ।
प्राक्सम्भवं न च रतं नहि वस्तु किञ्चित्
ज्ञानामृतं समरसं गगनोपमोऽहम् ॥

nirbhinna-bhinna-rahitaṁ paramārtha-tattvam
antar-bahir-na hi kathaṁ paramārtha-tattvam,
prāk-sambhavaṁ na ca rataṁ nahi vastu kiñchit
jñānāmṛtaṁ samarasaṁ gaganopamo'ham.

The Supreme Truth is beyond Undivided and Divided.
The Supreme Truth is beyond Within and Without.
Beyond Causation, Attachment, and Objectivity,
Essence of Wisdom, Serene Blissfulness,
Infinite as Space am I.

3.19

रागादिदोषरहितं त्वहमेव तत्त्वं
दैवादिदोषरहितं त्वहमेव तत्त्वम् ।
संसारशोकरहितं त्वहमेव तत्त्वं
ज्ञानामृतं समरसं गगनोपमोऽहम् ॥

rāgādi-doṣa-rahitaṁ twaham-eva tattvaṁ
daivādi-doṣa-rahitaṁ twaham-eva tattvam,
samsāra-śoka-rahitaṁ twaham-eva tattvaṁ
jñānāmṛtaṁ samarasaṁ gaganopamo'ham.

Free of the fault of Attachment I am truly the Essence.
Free of the fault of Destiny I am truly the Essence.
Free of the sorrows of Samsara I am truly the Essence.
Essence of Wisdom, Serene Blissfulness,
Infinite as Space am I.

3.20

स्थानत्रयं यदि च नेति कथं तुरीयं
कालत्रयं यदि च नेति कथं दिशश्च ।
शान्तं पदं हि परमं परमार्थतत्त्वं
ज्ञानामृतं समरसं गगनोपमोऽहम् ॥

sthāna-trayaṁ yadi ca neti kathaṁ turīyaṁ
kāla-trayaṁ yadi ca neti kathaṁ diśaśca,
śāntaṁ padaṁ hi paramaṁ paramārtha-tattvaṁ
jñānāmṛtaṁ samarasaṁ gaganopamo'ham.

If there are not the three States of Consciousness,
How can there be the fourth?
If there are not the three Divisions of Time,
How can there be the four Directions?
I am the Very Abode of Peace, the Supreme Reality.
Essence of Wisdom, Serene Blissfulness,
Infinite as Space am I.

3.21

दीर्घो लघुः पुनरितीह नमे विभागो
विस्तारसंकटमितीह न मे विभागः ।
कोणं हि वर्तुलमितीह न मे विभागो
ज्ञानामृतं समरसं गगनोपमोऽहम् ॥

dīrgho laghuḥ punar-itīha name vibhāgo
vistāra-saṅkaṭam-itīha na me vibhāgaḥ,
koṇaṁ hi vartulam-itīha na me vibhāgo
jñānāmṛtaṁ samarasaṁ gaganopamo'ham.

I cannot be defined as Long or Short,
I cannot be defined as Broad or Narrow,
I cannot be defined as Angular or Circular,
Essence of Wisdom, Serene Blissfulness,
Infinite as Space am I.

3.22

मातापितादि तनयादि न मे कदाचित्
जातं मृतं न च मनो न च मे कदाचित् ।
निर्व्याकुलं स्थिरमिदं परमार्थतत्त्वं
ज्ञानामृतं समरसं गगनोपमोऽहम् ॥

mātā-pitādi tanayādi na me kadācit
jātaṁ mṛtaṁ na ca mano na ca me kadācit,
nirvyākulaṁ sthiram-idaṁ paramārtha-tattvaṁ
jñānāmṛtaṁ samarasaṁ gaganopamo'ham.

Never have I had a Father, Mother, or Child.
Never have I had Birth, Death, or Mind.
I am Serene and Stable, the Supreme Reality.
Essence of Wisdom, Serene Blissfulness,
Infinite as Space am I.

3.23

शुद्धं विशुद्धमविचारमनन्तरूपं
निर्लेपलेपमविचारमनन्तरूपम् ।
निष्खण्डखण्डमविचारमनन्तरूपं
ज्ञानामृतं समरसं गगनोपमोऽहम् ॥

śuddhaṁ viśuddham-avicāram-ananta-rūpaṁ
nirlepa-lepam-avicāram-ananta-rūpam,
niṣkhaṇḍa-khaṇḍam-avicāram-ananta-rūpaṁ
jñānāmṛtaṁ samarasaṁ gaganopamo'ham.

I am Pure, Very Pure, beyond Thought, of Infinite form.
Unattached and Attached, beyond Thought, of Infinite form.
Undivided and Divided, beyond Thought, of Infinite form.
Essence of Wisdom, Serene Blissfulness,
Infinite as Space am I.

3.24

ब्रह्मादयः सुरगणाः कथमत्र सन्ति
स्वर्गादयो वसतयः कथमत्र सन्ति ।
यद्येकरूपममलं परमार्थतत्त्वं
ज्ञानामृतं समरसं गगनोपमोऽहम् ॥

brahmādayaḥ sura-gaṇāḥ katham-atra santi
swargādayo vasatayaḥ katham-atra santi,
yadyekarūpam-amalaṁ paramārtha-tattvaṁ
jñānāmṛtaṁ samarasaṁ gaganopamo'ham.

If the Supreme Truth is One and Pure,
How can there be Brahma and the Gods?
How can there be Abodes such as the Heavens?
Essence of Wisdom, Serene Blissfulness,
Infinite as Space am I.

3.25

निर्नेति नेति विमलो हि कथं वदामि
निःशेषशेषविमलो हि कथं वदामि ।
निर्लिङ्गलिङ्गविमलो हि कथं वदामि
ज्ञानामृतं समरसं गगनोपमोऽहम् ॥

nirneti neti vimalo hi kathaṁ vadāmi
niśśeṣa-śeṣa-vimalo hi kathaṁ vadāmi,
nirliṅga-liṅga-vimalo hi kathaṁ vadāmi
jñānāmṛtaṁ samarasaṁ gaganopamo'ham.

The Pure One which is "not this and not not this",
How shall I speak of It?
The Pure One which is Infinite and Finite,
How shall I speak of It?
The Pure One which is with and without Attributes,
How shall I speak of It?
Essence of Wisdom, Serene Blissfulness,
Infinite as Space am I.

3.26

निष्कर्मकर्मपरमं सततं करोमि
निःसङ्गसङ्गरहितं परमं विनोदम् ।
निर्देहदेहरहितं सततं विनोदं
ज्ञानामृतं समरसं गगनोपमोऽहम् ॥

niṣkarma-karma-paramaṁ satataṁ karomi
nissaṅga-saṅga-rahitaṁ paramaṁ vinodam,
nirdeha-deha-rahitaṁ satataṁ vinodaṁ
jñānāmṛtaṁ samarasaṁ gaganopamo'ham.

Free of Action, I perform the Supreme Action.
Free of Non-attachment and Attachment,
I am Supreme Bliss.
Free of Bodilessness and Body,
I am Eternal Bliss.
Essence of Wisdom, Serene Blissfulness,
Infinite as Space am I.

3.27

मायाप्रपञ्चरचना न च मे विकारः
कौटिल्यदम्भरचना न च मे विकारः ।
सत्यानृतेति रचना न च मे विकारो
ज्ञानामृतं समरसं गगनोपमोऽहम् ॥

māyā-prapañca-racanā na ca me vikāraḥ
kauṭilya-daṁbha-racanā na ca me vikāraḥ,
satyānṛteti-racanā na ca me vikāraḥ
jñānāmṛtaṁ samarasaṁ gaganopamo'ham.

This Play of Maya does not cause a Change in Me.
Falsehood and Fraud do not cause a Change in Me.
Truth and Untruth do not cause a Change in Me.
Essence of Wisdom, Serene Blissfulness,
Infinite as Space am I.

3.28

सन्ध्यादिकालरहितं न च मे वियोगो
ह्यन्तः प्रबोधरहितं बधिरो न मूकः ।
एवं विकल्परहितं न च भावशुद्धं
ज्ञानामृतं समरसं गगनोपमोऽहम् ॥

sandhyādi-kāla-rahitaṁ na ca me viyogo
hyantaḥ prabodha-rahitaṁ badhiro na mūkaḥ,
evaṁ vikalpa-rahitaṁ na ca bhāva-śuddhaṁ
jñānāmṛtaṁ samarasaṁ gaganopamo'ham.

Beyond Divisions of Time such as dusk, I am never astray.
Beyond Inner Awakening, I am neither deaf nor mute.
Beyond Doubt, I am not purified by mental attitudes.
Essence of Wisdom, Serene Blissfulness,
Infinite as Space am I.

3.29

निर्नाथनाथरहितं हि निराकुलं वै
निश्चित्तचित्तविगतं हि निराकुलं वै ।
संविद्धि सर्वविगतं हि निराकुलं वै
ज्ञानामृतं समरसं गगनोपमोऽहम् ॥

nirnātha-nātha-rahitaṁ hi nirākulaṁ vai
niścitta-citta-vigataṁ hi nirākulaṁ vai,
saṁviddhi sarva-vigataṁ hi nirākulaṁ vai
jñānāmṛtaṁ samarasaṁ gaganopamo'ham.

Independent of not having or having a Master,
I am Composed.
Independent of not having or having a Mind,
I am Composed.
Transcending all Duality,
I am Composed.
Essence of Wisdom, Serene Blissfulness,
Infinite as Space am I.

3.30

कान्तारमन्दिरमिदं हि कथं वदामि
संसिद्धसंशयमिदं हि कथं वदामि ।
एवं निरन्तरसमं हि निराकुलं वै
ज्ञानामृतं समरसं गगनोपमोऽहम् ॥

kāntāra-mandiram-idaṁ hi kathaṁ vadāmi
saṁsiddha-saṁśayam-idaṁ hi kathaṁ vadāmi,
evaṁ nirantara-samaṁ hi nirākulaṁ vai
jñānāmṛtaṁ samarasaṁ gaganopamo'ham.

Forest or temple, what should I say It is?
Validated or dubious, what should I say It is?
It is One Indivisible Sameness, and Poised.
Essence of Wisdom, Serene Blissfulness,
Infinite as Space am I.

3.31

निर्जीवजीवरहितं सततं विभाति
निर्बीजबीजरहितं सततं विभाति ।
निर्वाणबन्धरहितं सततं विभाति
ज्ञानामृतं समरसं गगनोपमोऽहम् ॥

nirjīva-jīva-rahitaṁ satataṁ vibhāti
nirbīja-bīja-rahitaṁ satataṁ vibhāti,
nirvāṇa-bandha-rahitaṁ satataṁ vibhāti
jñānāmṛtaṁ samarasaṁ gaganopamo'ham.

Free of Insentience and Sentience, It Shines Eternally.
Free of Causeless-ness and Cause, It Shines Eternally.
Free of Liberation and Bondage, It Shines Eternally.
Essence of Wisdom, Serene Blissfulness,
Infinite as Space am I.

3.32

सम्भूतिवर्जितमिदं सततं विभाति
संसारवर्जितमिदं सततं विभाति ।
संहारवर्जितमिदं सततं विभाति
ज्ञानामृतं समरसं गगनोपमोऽहम् ॥

saṁbhūti-varjitam-idaṁ satataṁ vibhāti
saṁsāra-varjitam-idaṁ satataṁ vibhāti,
saṁhāra-varjitam-idaṁ satataṁ vibhāti
jñānāmṛtaṁ samarasaṁ gaganopamo'ham.

Unrestrained by an Origin, It Shines Eternally.
Unrestrained by Samsara, It Shines Eternally.
Unrestrained by Destruction, It Shines Eternally.
Essence of Wisdom, Serene Blissfulness,
Infinite as Space am I.

3.33

उल्लेखमात्रमपि ते न च नामरूपं
निर्भिन्नभिन्नमपि ते न हि वस्तु किञ्चित् ।
निर्लज्जमानस करोषि कथं विषादं
ज्ञानामृतं समरसं गगनोपमोऽहम् ॥

ullekhamātram-api te na ca nāma-rūpaṁ
nirbhinna-bhinnam-api te na hi vastu kiñchit,
nirlajja-mānasa karoṣi kathaṁ viṣādaṁ
jñānāmṛtaṁ samarasaṁ gaganopamo'ham.

You have No Name or Form, even by Implication.
No object is the Same or Different from you.
Why do you Sorrow, O Wanton Mind?
Essence of Wisdom, Serene Blissfulness,
Infinite as Space am I.

3.34

किं नाम रोदिषि सखे न जरा न मृत्युः
किं नाम रोदिषि सखे न च जन्म दुःखम् ।
किं नाम रोदिषि सखे न च ते विकारो
ज्ञानामृतं समरसं गगनोपमोऽहम् ॥

kiṁ nāma rodiṣi sakhe na jarā na mṛtyuḥ
kiṁ nāma rodiṣi sakhe na ca janma duḥkham,
kiṁ nāma rodiṣi sakhe na ca te vikāraḥ
jñānāmṛtaṁ samarasaṁ gaganopamo'ham.

For what do you weep My Friend,
There is no Old Age or Death in you.
For what do you weep My Friend,
There is no Pain of birth in you.
For what do you weep My Friend,
There is no Modification in you.
Essence of Wisdom, Serene Blissfulness,
Infinite as Space am I.

3.35

किं नाम रोदिषि सखे न च ते स्वरूपं
किं नाम रोदिषि सखे न च ते विरूपम् ।
किं नाम रोदिषि सखे न च ते वयांसि
ज्ञानामृतं समरसं गगनोपमोऽहम् ॥

kiṁ nāma rodiṣi sakhe na ca te swarūpaṁ
kiṁ nāma rodiṣi sakhe na ca te virūpam,
kiṁ nāma rodiṣi sakhe na ca te vayāṁsi
jñānāmṛtaṁ samarasaṁ gaganopamo'ham.

What is the reason that you weep My Friend,
You have no Form in you.
What is the reason that you weep My Friend,
You have no Deformity in you.
What is the reason that you weep My Friend,
You have no Decline in you.
Essence of Wisdom, Serene Blissfulness,
Infinite as Space am I.

3.36

किं नाम रोदिषि सखे न च ते वयांसि
किं नाम रोदिषि सखे न च ते मनांसि ।
किं नाम रोदिषि सखे न तवेन्द्रियाणि
ज्ञानामृतं समरसं गगनोपमोऽहम् ॥

kiṁ nāma rodiṣi sakhe na ca te vayāṁsi
kiṁ nāma rodiṣi sakhe na ca te manāṁsi,
kiṁ nāma rodiṣi sakhe na tavendriyāṇi
jñānāmṛtaṁ samarasaṁ gaganopamo'ham.

Why do you weep My Friend,
You can never Wane.
Why do you weep My Friend,
You have no Mind.
Why do you weep My Friend,
You have no Senses.
Essence of Wisdom, Serene Blissfulness,
Infinite as Space am I.

3.37

किं नाम रोदिषि सखे न च तेऽस्ति कामः
किं नाम रोदिषि सखे न च ते प्रलोभः ।
किं नाम रोदिषि सखे न च ते विमोहो
ज्ञानामृतं समरसं गगनोपमोऽहम् ॥

kiṁ nāma rodiṣi sakhe na ca te'sti kāmaḥ
kiṁ nāma rodiṣi sakhe na ca te pralobhaḥ,
kiṁ nāma rodiṣi sakhe na ca te vimoho
jñānāmṛtaṁ samarasaṁ gaganopamo'ham.

For what do you weep My Friend,
You have no Lust in you.
For what do you weep My Friend,
You have no Greed in you.
For what do you weep My Friend,
You have no Temptation in you.
Essence of Wisdom, Serene Blissfulness,
Infinite as Space am I.

3.38

ऐश्वर्यमिच्छसि कथं न च ते धनानि
ऐश्वर्यमिच्छसि कथं न च ते हि पत्नी ।
ऐश्वर्यमिच्छसि कथं न च ते ममेति
ज्ञानामृतं समरसं गगनोपमोऽहम् ॥

aiśvaryam-icchasi kathaṁ na ca te dhanāni
aiśvaryam-icchasi kathaṁ na ca te hi patnī,
aiśvaryam-icchasi kathaṁ na ca te mameti
jñānāmṛtaṁ samarasaṁ gaganopamo'ham.

Why do you desire Influence, you have no Wealth.
Why do you desire Influence, you have no Wife.
Why do you desire Influence, you have no sense of Mine.
Essence of Wisdom, Serene Blissfulness,
Infinite as Space am I.

3.39

लिङ्गप्रपञ्चजनुषी न च ते न मे च
निर्लज्जमानसमिदं च विभाति भिन्नम् ।
निर्भेदभेदरहितं न च ते न मे च
ज्ञानामृतं समरसं गगनोपमोऽहम् ॥

liṅga-prapañca-januṣī na ca te na me ca
nirlajja-mānasam-idaṁ ca vibhāti bhinnam,
nirbheda-bheda-rahitaṁ na ca te na me ca
jñānāmṛtaṁ samarasaṁ gaganopamo'ham.

This disguise of a World born of Illusion
Is neither yours nor mine.
It is the wanton mind that sees Multiplicity.
You and I are free of Division and Non-Division.
Essence of Wisdom, Serene Blissfulness,
Infinite as Space am I.

3.40

नो वाणुमात्रमपि ते हि विरागरूपं
नो वाणुमात्रमपि ते हि सरागरूपम् ।
नो वाणुमात्रमपि ते हि सकामरूपं
ज्ञानामृतं समरसं गगनोपमोऽहम् ॥

no vāṇumātram-api te hi virāga-rūpaṁ
no vāṇumātram-api te hi sarāga-rūpam,
no vāṇumātram-api te hi sakāma-rūpaṁ
jñānāmṛtaṁ samarasaṁ gaganopamo'ham.

Not even a hint of Detachment exists in you.
Not even a hint of Attachment exists in you.
Not even a hint of Desire exists in you.
Essence of Wisdom, Serene Blissfulness,
Infinite as Space am I.

3.41

ध्याता न ते हि हृदये न च ते समाधि-
र्ध्यानं न ते हि हृदये न बहिः प्रदेशः ।
ध्येयं न चेति हृदये न हि वस्तु कालो
ज्ञानामृतं समरसं गगनोपमोऽहम् ॥

dhyātā na te hi hṛdaye na ca te samādhir-
dhyānaṁ na te hi hṛdaye na bahiḥ pradeśaḥ,
dhyeyaṁ na ceti hṛdaye na hi vastu kālo
jñānāmṛtaṁ samarasaṁ gaganopamo'ham.

There is no Meditator in your heart,
Nor is there Samadhi.
There is no Meditation in your heart,
Nor is there the Outside World.
There is no one to Meditate upon in your heart,
Nor any Object nor Time.
Essence of Wisdom, Serene Blissfulness,
Infinite as Space am I.

3.42

यत्सारभूतमखिलं कथितं मया ते
न त्वं न मे न महतो न गुरुर्न शिष्यः ।
स्वच्छन्दरूपसहजं परमार्थतत्त्वं
ज्ञानामृतं समरसं गगनोपमोऽहम् ॥

yat-sārabhūtam-akhilaṁ kathitaṁ mayā te
na twaṁ na me na mahato na guruṛ-na śiṣyaḥ,
swacchanda-rūpa-sahajaṁ paramārtha-tattvaṁ
jñānāmṛtaṁ samarasaṁ gaganopamo'ham.

I have told you the Essence of the Whole Truth.
There is no You, nor Me,
No Superior Being, no Guru, and no Disciple.
The Ultimate Reality is Innate and Natural.
Essence of Wisdom, Serene Blissfulness,
Infinite as Space am I.

3.43

कथमिह परमार्थं तत्त्वमानन्दरूपं
कथमिह परमार्थं नैवमानन्दरूपम् ।
कथमिह परमार्थं ज्ञानविज्ञानरूपं
यदि परमहमेकं वर्तते व्योमरूपम् ॥

katham-iha paramārthaṁ tattvam-ānanda-rūpaṁ
katham-iha paramārthaṁ naivam-ānanda-rūpam,
katham-iha paramārthaṁ jñāna-vijñāna- rūpaṁ
yadi param-aham-ekaṁ vartate vyoma-rūpam.

How is the Supreme Reality of the nature of Bliss?
How is the Supreme Reality not of the nature of Bliss?
How is the Supreme Reality
Of the nature of Knowledge and Wisdom,
If I, the Supreme Alone Exists, of the Nature of Space?

3.44

दहनपवनहीनं विद्धि विज्ञानमेक-
मवनिजलविहीनं विद्धि विज्ञानरूपम् ।
समगमनविहीनं विद्धि विज्ञानमेकं
गगनमिव विशालं विद्धि विज्ञानमेकम् ॥

dahana-pavana-hīnaṁ viddhi vijñānam-ekaṁ
avani-jala-vihīnaṁ viddhi vijñāna-rūpam,
sama-gamana-vihīnaṁ viddhi vijñānam-ekaṁ
gaganam-iva viśālaṁ viddhi vijñānam-ekam.

Know the One Awareness
That is free of Fire and Air.
Know the One Awareness
That is free of Earth and Water.
Know the One Awareness
That is beyond all Coming and Going.
Know the One Awareness that is Vast as Space.

3.45

न शून्यरूपं न विशून्यरूपं
न शुद्धरूपं न विशुद्धरूपम् ।
रूपं विरूपं न भवामि किञ्चित्
स्वरूपरूपं परमार्थतत्त्वम् ॥

na śūnya-rūpaṁ na viśunya-rūpaṁ
na śuddha-rūpaṁ na viśuddha-rūpam,
rūpaṁ virūpaṁ na bhavāmi kiñcit
swarūpa-rūpaṁ paramārtha-tattvam.

I am not of the nature of Emptiness,
Nor of the nature of Non-Emptiness.
I am not of the nature of Purity,
Nor of the nature of Impurity.
I am neither Beautiful nor Deformed, in the least.
I am the Supreme Reality of the Form of Itself.

3.46

मुञ्च मुञ्च हि संसारं त्यागं मुञ्च हि सर्वथा ।
त्यागात्यागविषं शुद्धममृतं सहजं ध्रुवम् ॥

muñca muñca hi saṁsāraṁ tyāgaṁ muñca hi sarvathā,
tyāgātyāga-viṣaṁ śuddham-amṛtaṁ sahajaṁ dhruvam.

Renounce, Renounce Samsara!
Then Renounce Renunciation as well!
Both Renunciation and Acceptance are Poisons.
You are Pure, Immortal, Natural, and Changeless.

Chapter 4

The Wise drink of the Nectar of Renunciation

4.1

नावाहनं नैव विसर्जनं वा
पुष्पाणि पत्राणि कथं भवन्ति ।
ध्यानानि मन्त्राणि कथं भवन्ति
समासमं चैव शिवार्चनं च ॥

nāvāhanaṁ naiva visarjanaṁ vā
puṣpāṇi patrāṇi kathaṁ bhavanti,
dhyānāni mantrāṇi kathaṁ bhavanti
samāsamaṁ caiva śivārcanaṁ ca.

How can there be Invocation
Or ritualistic Idol Dissolution,
Offerings of flowers and leaves,
Meditation and Japa,
To Śiva, who is both One and Many?

4.2

न केवलं बन्धविबन्धमुक्तो
न केवलं शुद्धविशुद्धमुक्तः ।
न केवलं योगवियोगमुक्तः
स वै विमुक्तो गगनोपमोऽहम् ॥

na kevalaṁ bandha-vibandha-mukto
na kevalaṁ śuddha-viśuddha-muktaḥ,
na kevalaṁ yoga-viyoga-muktaḥ
sa vai vimukto gaganopamo'ham.

Not only am I free of Bondage and Liberation,
Purity and Impurity,
Union and Separation,
I am Truly Free and Infinite like Space.

4.3

सञ्जायते सर्वमिदं हि तथ्यं
सञ्जायते सर्वमिदं वितथ्यम् ।
एवं विकल्पो मम नैव जातः
स्वरूपनिर्वाणमनामयोऽहम् ॥

sañjāyate sarvam-idaṁ hi tathyaṁ
sañjāyate sarvam-idaṁ vitathyam,
evaṁ vikalpo mama naiva jātaḥ
swarūpa-nirvāṇam-anāmayo'ham.

This Creation is the Truth,
This Creation is not the Truth,
Such doubts do not arise in me.
Unfettered by Maya, Freedom is My Very Nature.

4.4

न साञ्जनं चैव निरञ्जनं वा
न चान्तरं वापि निरन्तरं वा ।
अन्तर्विभन्नं न हि मे विभाति
स्वरूपनिर्वाणमनामयोऽहम् ॥

na sāñjanaṁ caiva nirañjanaṁ vā
na cāntaraṁ vāpi nirantaraṁ vā,
antarvibhinnaṁ na hi me vibhāti
swarūpa-nirvāṇam-anāmayo'ham.

Neither Blemished nor Unblemished,
Neither Discontinuous nor Continuous,
Nor any Divisions do I see.
Unfettered by Maya, Freedom is My Very Nature.

4.5

अबोधबोधो मम नैव जातो
बोधस्वरूपं मम नैव जातम् ।
निर्बोधबोधं च कथं वदामि
स्वरूपनिर्वाणमनामयोऽहम् ॥

abodha-bodho mama naiva jāto
bodha-swarūpaṁ mama naiva jātam,
nirbodha-bodhaṁ ca kathaṁ vadāmi
swarūpa-nirvāṇam-anāmayo'ham.

Ignorance or Knowledge does not arise in me.
Self-knowledge does not arise in me.
How can I say I have Ignorance or Knowledge,
Unfettered by Maya, Freedom is My Very Nature.

4.6

न धर्मयुक्तो न च पापयुक्तो
न बन्धयुक्तो न च मोक्षयुक्तः ।
युक्तं त्वयुक्तं न च मे विभाति
स्वरूपनिर्वाणमनामयोऽहम् ॥

na dharma-yukto na ca pāpa-yukto
na bandha-yukto na ca mokṣa-yuktaḥ,
yuktaṁ tvayuktaṁ na ca me vibhāti
swarūpa-nirvāṇam-anāmayo'ham.

Neither yoked with Righteousness nor Sin,
Neither yoked with Bondage nor Freedom,
Neither Union nor Separation do I see,
Unfettered by Maya, Freedom is My Very Nature.

4.7

परापरं वा न च मे कदाचित्
मध्यस्थभावो हि न चारिमित्रम् ।
हिताहितं चापि कथं वदामि
स्वरूपनिर्वाणमनामयोऽहम् ॥

parāparaṁ vā na ca me kadācit
madhyastha-bhāvo hi na cāri-mitram,
hitāhitaṁ cāpi kathaṁ vadāmi
swarūpa-nirvāṇam-anāmayo'ham.

None is ever Superior or Inferior to me.
I am neither Neutral nor have I Foe nor Friend.
How then, shall I speak of Good or Evil?
Unfettered by Maya, Freedom is My Very Nature.

4.8

नोपासको नैवमुपास्यरूपं
न चोपदेशो न च मे क्रिया च ।
संवित्स्वरूपं च कथं वदामि
स्वरूपनिर्वाणमनामयोऽहम् ॥

nopāsako naivam-upāsya-rūpaṁ
na copadeśo na ca me kriyā ca,
saṁvit-swarūpaṁ ca kathaṁ vadāmi
swarūpa-nirvāṇam anāmayo'ham.

I am neither the Worshipper nor the Worshipped.
I have neither Instruction nor Practice.
What shall I say of my nature, which is Consciousness?
Unfettered by Maya, Freedom is My Very Nature.

4.9

नो व्यापकं व्याप्यमिहास्ति किञ्चित्
न चालयं वापि निरालयं वा ।
अशून्यशून्यं च कथं वदामि
स्वरूपनिर्वाणमनामयोऽहम् ॥

no vyāpakaṁ vyāpyam-ihāsti kiñchit
na cālayaṁ vāpi nirālayaṁ vā,
aśūnya-śūnyaṁ ca kathaṁ vadāmi
swarūpa-nirvāṇam-anāmayo'ham.

Nothing here Pervades or is Pervaded.
It has no Place, nor is It Place-less.
How then shall I explain It as Non-Emptiness or Emptiness?
Unfettered by Maya, Freedom is My Very Nature.

4.10

न ग्राहको ग्राह्यकमेव किञ्चित्
न कारणं वा मम नैव कार्यम् ।
अचिन्त्यचिन्त्यं च कथं वदामि
स्वरूपनिर्वाणमनामयोऽहम् ॥

na grāhako grāhyakam-eva kiñchit
na kāraṇaṁ vā mama naiva kāryam,
acintya-cintyaṁ ca kathaṁ vadāmi
swarūpa-nirvāṇam-anāmayo'ham.

I am neither Subject nor Object,
Neither Cause nor Effect,
How can I say,
I am Comprehensible or Incomprehensible?
Unfettered by Maya, Freedom is My Very Nature.

4.11

न भेदकं वापि न चैव भेद्यं
न वेदकं वा मम नैव वेद्यम् ।
गतागतं तात कथं वदामि
स्वरूपनिर्वाणमनामयोऽहम् ॥

na bhedakaṁ vāpi na caiva bhedyaṁ
na vedakaṁ vā mama naiva vedyam,
gatāgataṁ tāta kathaṁ vadāmi
swarūpa-nirvāṇam-anāmayo'ham.

I neither Differentiate nor am I Differentiated,
Neither Knower nor Knowable,
How should I speak of Creation and Dissolution, My Child?
Unfettered by Maya, Freedom is My Very Nature.

4.12

न चास्ति देहो न च मे विदेहो
बुद्धिर्मनो मे न हि चेन्द्रियाणि ।
रागो विरागश्च कथं वदामि
स्वरूपनिर्वाणमनामयोऽहम् ॥

na cāsti deho na ca me videho
buddhir-mano me na hi cendriyāṇi,
rāgo virāgaś-ca kathaṁ vadāmi
swarūpa-nirvāṇam-anāmayo'ham.

I neither have a Body nor am I Bodiless.
Nor have I Intellect, Mind nor Senses.
How then shall I speak of Attachment and Aversion?
Unfettered by Maya, Freedom is My Very Nature.

4.13

उल्लेखमात्रं न हि भिन्नमुच्चै-
रुल्लेखमात्रं न तिरोहितं वै ।
समासमं मित्र कथं वदामि
स्वरूपनिर्वाणमनामयोऽहम् ॥

ullekha-mātraṁ na hi bhinnam-uccaiḥ
ullekha-mātraṁ na tirohitaṁ vai,
samāsamaṁ mitra kathaṁ vadāmi
swarūpa-nirvāṇam-anāmayo'ham.

One cannot even mention a thing Separate from It.
One cannot even mention It as Concealed.
Friend, how then, shall I speak of Similar or Dissimilar?
Unfettered by Maya, Freedom is My Very Nature.

4.14

जितेन्द्रियोऽहं त्वजितेन्द्रियो वा
न संयमो मे नियमो न जातः ।
जयाजयौ मित्र कथं वदामि
स्वरूपनिर्वाणमनामयोऽहम् ॥

jitendriyo'haṁ tvajitendriyo vā
na saṁyamo me niyamo na jātaḥ,
jayājayau mitra kathaṁ vadāmi
swarūpa-nirvāṇam-anāmayo'ham.

I have neither Subdued
Nor Not Subdued the Senses.
Neither have I Self-Control nor Discipline.
Friend, how then, shall I speak of Victory or Defeat?
Unfettered by Maya, Freedom is My Very Nature.

4.15

अमूर्तमूर्तिर्न च मे कदाचि-
दाद्यन्तमध्यं न च मे कदाचित् ।
बलाबलं मित्र कथं वदामि
स्वरूपनिर्वाणमनामयोऽहम् ॥

amūrta-mūrtir-na ca me kadācit
ādy-anta-madhyaṁ na ca me kadācit,
balābalaṁ mitra kathaṁ vadāmi
swarūpa-nirvāṇam-anāmayo'ham.

Devoid of Form and Formlessness,
Devoid of Beginning, Middle, and End,
Friend, how then, shall I speak of Strength and Weakness?
Unfettered by Maya, Freedom is My Very Nature.

4.16

मृतामृतं वापि विषाविषं च
सञ्जायते तात न मे कदाचित् ।
अशुद्धशुद्धं च कथं वदामि
स्वरूपनिर्वाणमनामयोऽहम् ॥

mṛtāmṛtaṁ vāpi viṣāviṣaṁ ca
sañjāyate tāta na me kadācit,
aśuddha-śuddhaṁ ca kathaṁ vadāmi
swarūpa-nirvāṇam-anāmayo'ham.

Mortality and Immortality, Evil and Good,
Never Arise in Me, My Child.
How then, shall I speak of Impurity and Purity?
Unfettered by Maya, Freedom is My Very Nature.

4.17

स्वप्नः प्रबोधो न च योगमुद्रा
नक्तं दिवा वापि न मे कदाचित् ।
अतुर्यतुर्यं च कथं वदामि
स्वरूपनिर्वाणमनामयोऽहम् ॥

swapnaḥ prabodho na ca yoga-mudra
naktaṁ divā vāpi na me kadācit,
aturya-turyaṁ ca kathaṁ vadāmi
swarūpa-nirvāṇam-anāmayo'ham.

I have never known Dreaming nor Waking,
Neither Yogic Postures nor Day and Night,
How then, shall I speak of Transcendental and Relative States?
Unfettered by Maya, Freedom is My Very Nature.

4.18

संविद्धि मां सर्वविसर्वमुक्तं
माया विमाया न च मे कदाचित् ।
सन्ध्यादिकं कर्म कथं वदामि
स्वरूपनिर्वाणमनामयोऽहम् ॥

saṁviddhi māṁ sarva-visarva-muktaṁ
māyā-vimāyā na ca me kadācit,
sandhyādikaṁ karma kathaṁ vadāmi
swarūpa-nirvāṇam-anāmayo'ham.

Know that I am Free of Everything and Nothing.
I am Free of Maya and its Different Forms.
How then, shall I speak of Daily Rituals?
Unfettered by Maya, Freedom is My Very Nature.

4.19

संविद्धि मां सर्वसमाधियुक्तं
संविद्धि मां लक्ष्यविलक्ष्यमुक्तम् ।
योगं वियोगं च कथं वदामि
स्वरूपनिर्वाणमनामयोऽहम् ॥

saṁviddhi māṁ sarva-samādhi-yuktaṁ
saṁviddhi māṁ lakṣya-vilakṣya-muktam,
yogaṁ viyogaṁ ca kathaṁ vadāmi
swarūpa-nirvāṇam-anāmayo'ham.

Know that I am Fully Absorbed in Samadhi.
Know that I am Free of Ambition and Idleness.
How then, shall I speak of Union and Separation?
Unfettered by Maya, Freedom is My Very Nature.

4.20

मूर्खोऽपि नाहं न च पण्डितोऽहं
मौनं विमौनं न च मे कदाचित् ।
तर्कं वितर्कं च कथं वदामि
स्वरूपनिर्वाणमनामयोऽहम् ॥

mūrkho'pi nāhaṁ na ca panḍito'haṁ
maunaṁ vimaunaṁ na ca me kadācit,
tarkaṁ vitarkaṁ ca kathaṁ vadāmi
swarūpa-nirvāṇam-anāmayo'ham.

I am neither Unlearned nor Learned,
Neither Silent nor Communicative,
How then, shall I speak of Argumentation?
Unfettered by Maya, Freedom is My Very Nature.

4.21

पिता च माता च कुलं न जाति-
र्जन्मादि मृत्युर्न च मे कदाचित् ।
स्नेहं विमोहं च कथं वदामि
स्वरूपनिर्वाणमनामयोऽहम् ॥

pitā ca mātā ca kulaṁ na jātiḥ
janmādi mṛtyur-na ca me kadācit,
snehaṁ vimohaṁ ca kathaṁ vadāmi
swarūpa-nirvāṇam-anāmayo'ham.

Never have I had a Father or a Mother,
Family or Caste, Birth or Death.
How then, shall I speak of Affection or Delusion?
Unfettered by Maya, Freedom is My Very Nature.

4.22

अस्तं गतो नैव सदोदितोऽहं
तेजोवितेजो न च मे कदाचित् ।
सन्ध्यादिकं कर्म कथं वदामि
स्वरूपनिर्वाणमनामयोऽहम् ॥

astaṁ gato naiva sadodito'haṁ
tejo-vitejo na ca me kadācit,
sandhyādikaṁ karma kathaṁ vadāmi
swarūpa-nirvāṇam-anāmayo'ham.

I am never gone, I am Always Existent.
Never is there Light nor Darkness in me.
How then, shall I speak of Daily Rituals?
Unfettered by Maya, Freedom is My Very Nature.

4.23

असंशयं विद्धि निराकुलं मां
असंशयं विद्धि निरन्तरं माम् ।
असंशयं विद्धि निरञ्जनं मां
स्वरूपनिर्वाणमनामयोऽहम् ॥

asaṁśayaṁ viddhi nirākulaṁ māṁ
asaṁśayaṁ viddhi nirantaraṁ mām,
asaṁśayaṁ viddhi nirañjanaṁ māṁ
swarūpa-nirvāṇam-anāmayo'ham.

With Certainty know that I am Serene.
With Certainty know that I am Eternal.
With Certainty know that I am Immaculate.
Unfettered by Maya, Freedom is My Very Nature.

4.24

ध्यानानि सर्वाणि परित्यजन्ति
शुभाशुभं कर्म परित्यजन्ति ।
त्यागामृतं तात पिबन्ति धीराः
स्वरूपनिर्वाणमनामयोऽहम् ॥

dhyānāni sarvāṇi parityajanti
śubhāśubhaṁ karma parityajanti,
tyāgāmṛtaṁ tāta pibanti dhīrāḥ
swarūpa-nirvāṇam-anāmayo'ham.

They Relinquish all Meditation,
They Relinquish all Good and Evil Deeds,
O Child, the Wise drink of the Nectar of Renunciation.
Unfettered by Maya, Freedom is My Very Nature.

4.25

विन्दति विन्दति न हि न हि यत्र
छन्दोलक्षणं न हि न हि तत्र ।
समरसमग्नो भावितपूतः
प्रलपति तत्त्वं परमवधूतः ॥

vindati vindati na hi na hi yatra
chando-lakṣaṇaṁ na hi na hi tatra,
samarasa-magno bhāvita-pūtaḥ
pralapati tattvaṁ param-avadhūtaḥ.

Where there is no Knowing
There can be no Verses.
Purified by Meditation,
Deeply absorbed in Absolute Equanimity,
The Avadhūta has spoken the Supreme Truth.

Chapter 5

Truth lies Beyond the Absolute and the Relative

5.1

ॐ इति गदितं गगनसमं तत्
न परापरसारविचार इति ।
अविलासविलासनिराकरणं
कथमक्षरबिन्दुसमुच्चरणम् ॥

Om iti gaditaṁ gagana-samaṁ tat
na parāpara-sāra-vicāra iti,
avilāsa-vilāsa-nirākaraṇaṁ
katham-akṣara-bindu-samuccaraṇam.

Om, the syllable, is All-Pervasive like the Sky.
Its truth lies beyond the Absolute and the Relative.
When both the Unmanifest and the Manifest are rejected,
What use is even a drop of Om Chanting?

5.2

इति तत्त्वमसिप्रभृतिश्रुतिभिः
प्रतिपादितमात्मनि तत्त्वमसि ।
त्वमुपाधिविवर्जितसर्वसमं
किमु रोदिषि मानसि सर्वसमम् ॥

iti tat-twam-asi-prabhṛti-śrutibhiḥ
pratipāditam-ātmani tat-tvam-asi,
twam-upādhi-vivarjita-sarva-samaṁ
kimu rodiṣi mānasi sarva-samam.

Scripture has declared, That Thou Art,
Establishing that You are the Only Reality.
Free of attributes, You are the Same Self in All.
Then why do you sorrow, O Mind,
You are the One Singular Truth of All Existence.

5.3

अध ऊर्ध्वविवर्जितसर्वसमं
बहिरन्तरवर्जितसर्वसमम् ।
यदि चैकविवर्जितसर्वसमं
किमु रोदिषि मानसि सर्वसमम् ॥

adha urdhva-vivarjita-sarva-samaṁ
bahirantara-varjita-sarva-samam,
yadi caikavivarjita-sarva-samaṁ
kimu rodiṣi mānasi sarva-samam.

Beyond Above and Below,
You are the Same Self in All.
Beyond Within and Without,
You are the Same Self in All.
Even beyond Singularity,
You are the Same Self in All.
Then why do you sorrow O Mind,
You are the One Singular Truth of All Existence.

5.4

न हि कल्पितकल्पविचार इति
न हि कारणकार्यविचार इति ।
पदसन्धिविवर्जितसर्वसमं
किमु रोदिषि मानसि सर्वसमम् ॥

na hi kalpita-kalpa-vicāra iti
na hi kāraṇa-kārya-vicāra iti,
pada-sandhi-vivarjita-sarva-samaṁ
kimu rodiṣi mānasi sarva-samam.

It cannot be known by Conceptuality and Intellection,
Nor by Cause and Effect.
Beyond Words and Word Combinations,
You are the Same Self in All.
Then why do you sorrow O Mind,
You are the One Singular Truth of All Existence.

5.5

न हि बोधविबोधसमाधिरिति
न हि देशविदेशसमाधिरिति ।
न हि कालविकालसमाधिरिति
किमु रोदिषि मानसि सर्वसमम् ॥

na hi bodha-vibodha-samādhir-iti
na hi deśa-videśa-samādhir-iti,
na hi kāla-vikāla-samādhir-iti
kimu rodiṣi mānasi sarva-samam.

The State of Oneness
Is Beyond Knowledge and Ignorance.
The State of Oneness
Is Beyond Nearness and Farness.
The State of Oneness
Is Beyond Time and Timelessness.
Then why do you sorrow O Mind,
You are the One Singular Truth of All Existence.

5.6

न हि कुम्भनभो न हि कुम्भ इति
न हि जीववपुर्न हि जीव इति ।
न हि कारणकार्यविभाग इति
किमु रोदिषि मानसि सर्वसमम् ॥

na hi kumbha-nabho na hi kumbha iti
na hi jīva-vapur-na hi jīva iti,
na hi kāraṇa-kārya-vibhāga iti
kimu rodiṣi mānasi sarva-samam.

There is neither Jar Space nor Jar,
Neither Body nor Individual,
Neither Distinction of Cause and Effect,
Then why do you sorrow O Mind,
You are the One Singular Truth of All Existence.

5.7

इह सर्वनिरन्तरमोक्षपदं
लघुदीर्घविचारविहीन इति ।
न हि वर्तुलकोणविभाग इति
किमु रोदिषि मानसि सर्वसमम् ॥

iha sarva-nirantara-mokṣa-padaṁ
laghu-dīrgha-vicāra-vihīna iti,
na hi vartula-koṇa-vibhāga iti
kimu rodiṣi mānasi sarva-samam.

It is the State of Freedom, All-Pervasive and Eternal.
There is no Distinction of Short and Long,
Circular and Angular.
Then why do you sorrow O Mind,
You are the One Singular Truth of All Existence.

5.8

इह शून्यविशून्यविहीन इति
इह शुद्धविशुद्धविहीन इति ।
इह सर्वविसर्वविहीन इति
किमु रोदिषि मानसि सर्वसमम् ॥

iha śūnya-viśūnya-vihīna iti
iha śhuddha-viśuddha-vihīna iti,
iha sarva-visarva-vihīna iti
kimu rodiṣi mānasi sarva-samam.

It is neither Emptiness nor Non-Emptiness.
It is neither Pure nor Impure.
It is neither Entire nor Partial.
Then why do you sorrow O Mind,
You are the One Singular Truth of All Existence.

5.9

न हि भिन्नविभिन्नविचार इति
बहिरन्तरसन्धिविचार इति ।
अरिमित्रविवर्जितसर्वसमं
किमु रोदिषि मानसि सर्वसमम् ॥

na hi bhinna-vibhinna-vicāra iti
bahir-antara-sandhi-vicāra iti,
ari-mitra-vivarjita-sarva-samaṁ
kimu rodiṣi mānasi sarva-samam.

It is neither Different nor Non-Different.
Neither Outside, Inside, nor their Junction.
Same in all, It is free of Foe and Friend.
Then why do you sorrow O Mind,
You are the One Singular Truth of All Existence.

5.10

न हि शिष्यविशिष्यस्वरूप इति
न चराचरभेदविचार इति ।
इह सर्वनिरन्तरमोक्षपदं
किमु रोदिषि मानसि सर्वसमम् ॥

na hi śiṣya-viśiṣya-swarūpa iti
na carācara-bheda-vicāra iti,
iha sarva-nirantara-mokṣa-padaṁ
kimu rodiṣi mānasi sarva-samam.

Free of the nature of Disciple or Non-Disciple,
Animate or Inanimate,
It is the State of Freedom, All-Pervasive and Eternal.
Then why do you sorrow O Mind,
You are the One Singular Truth of All Existence.

5.11

ननु रूपविरूपविहीन इति
ननु भिन्नविभिन्नविहीन इति ।
ननु सर्गविसर्गविहीन इति
किमु रोदिषि मानसि सर्वसमम् ॥

nanu rūpa-virūpa-vihīna iti
nanu bhinna-vibhinna-vihīna iti,
nanu sarga-visarga-vihīna iti
kimu rodiṣi mānasi sarva-samam.

Undoubtedly It is free of Form and Formlessness.
Undoubtedly It is free of Division and Non-Division.
Undoubtedly It is free of Creation and Dissolution.
Then why do you sorrow O Mind,
You are the One Singular Truth of All Existence.

5.12

न गुणागुणपाशनिबन्ध इति
मृतजीवनकर्म करोमि कथम् ।
इति शुद्धनिरञ्जनसर्वसमं
किमु रोदिषि मानसि सर्वसमम् ॥

na guṇāguṇa-pāśa-nibandha iti
mṛta-jīvana-karma karomi katham,
iti śuddha-nirañjana-sarva-samaṁ
kimu rodiṣi mānasi sarva-samam.

Not bound by the Chains of Virtue and Vice,
How then can I be bound by Life, Death, or Action?
I am The Pure Unblemished Self in All.
Then why do you sorrow O Mind,
You are the One Singular Truth of All Existence.

5.13

इह भावविभावविहीन इति
इह कामविकामविहीन इति ।
इह बोधतमं खलु मोक्षसमं
किमु रोदिषि मानसि सर्वसमम् ॥

iha bhāva-vibhāva-vihīna iti
iha kāma-vikāma-vihīna iti,
iha bodhatamaṁ khalu mokṣa-samaṁ
kimu rodiṣi mānasi sarva-samam.

Free of Emotion and the Causes of Emotion,
Transcending Desire and Desirelessness,
It is Pure Consciousness, which is Freedom.
Then why do you sorrow O Mind,
You are the One Singular Truth of All Existence.

5.14

इह तत्त्वनिरन्तरतत्त्वमिति
न हि सन्धिविसन्धिविहीन इति ।
यदि सर्वविवर्जितसर्वसमं
किमु रोदिषि मानसि सर्वसमम् ॥

iha tattva-nirantara-tattvam-iti
na hi sandhi-visandhi-vihīna-iti,
yadi sarva-vivarjita-sarva-samaṁ
kimu rodiṣi mānasi sarva-samam.

It Itself is the Ultimate Uninterrupted Truth.
It is devoid of Union and Separation.
When It is Independent of all, and the Same Self in All,
Then why do you sorrow O Mind,
You are the One Singular Truth of All Existence.

5.15

अनिकेतकुटी परिवारसमं
इहसङ्गविसङ्गविहीनपरम् ।
इह बोधविबोधविहीनपरं
किमु रोदिषि मानसि सर्वसमम् ॥

aniketa-kutī parivāra-samaṁ
iha-saṅga-visaṅga-vihīna-param,
iha bodha-vibodha-vihīna-paraṁ
kimu rodiṣi mānasi sarva-samam.

It is the Same Self in the homeless
And those with home and family.
Devoid of Attachment and Non-Attachment,
It is the Absolute Truth.
Devoid of Knowledge and Ignorance,
It is the Absolute Truth.
Then why do you sorrow O Mind,
You are the One Singular Truth of All Existence.

5.16

अविकारविकारमसत्यमिति
अविलक्षविलक्षमसत्यमिति ।
यदि केवलमात्मनि सत्यमिति
किमु रोदिषि मानसि सर्वसमम् ॥

avikāra-vikāram-asatyam-iti
avilakṣa-vilakṣam-asatyam-iti,
yadi kevalam-ātmani satyam-iti
kimu rodiṣi mānasi sarva-samam.

Change in the Unchanging One is Untruth.
Attribute in the Attribute-less One is Untruth.
When only the Self is Truth,
Then why do you sorrow O Mind,
You are the One Singular Truth of All Existence.

5.17

इह सर्वसमं खलु जीव इति
इह सर्वनिरन्तरजीव इति ।
इह केवलनिश्चलजीव इति
किमु रोदिषि मानसि सर्वसमम् ॥

iha sarva-samaṁ khalu jīva iti
iha sarva-nirantara-jīva iti,
iha kevala-niścala-jīva iti
kimu rodiṣi mānasi sarva-samam.

It indeed is the One Being in All.
It is the One Eternal Being in All.
It is the Only Unchanging Being.
Then why do you sorrow O Mind,
You are the One Singular Truth of All Existence.

5.18

अविवेकविवेकमबोध इति
अविकल्पविकल्पमबोध इति ।
यदि चैकनिरन्तरबोध इति
किमु रोदिषि मानसि सर्वसमम् ॥

aviveka-vivekam-abodha iti
avikalpa-vikalpam-abodha iti,
yadi caikanirantara-bodha iti
kimu rodiṣi mānasi sarva-samam.

Differentiating the Undifferentiated One is ignorance.
Doubting the One beyond doubt is ignorance.
When the One Indivisible Truth Alone is Knowledge,
Then why do you sorrow O Mind,
You are the One Singular Truth of All Existence.

5.19

न हि मोक्षपदं न हि बन्धपदं
न हि पुण्यपदं न हि पापपदम् ।
न हि पूर्णपदं न हि रिक्तपदं
किमु रोदिषि मानसि सर्वसमम् ॥

na hi mokṣa-padaṁ na hi bandha-padaṁ
na hi puṇya-padaṁ na hi pāpa-padam,
na hi pūrṇa-padaṁ na hi rikta-padaṁ
kimu rodiṣi mānasi sarva-samam.

There is No State of Freedom, there is No State of Bondage.
There is No State of Virtue, there is No State of Vice.
There is No State of Fullness, there is No State of Emptiness.
Then why do you sorrow O Mind,
You are the One Singular Truth of All Existence.

5.20

यदि वर्णविवर्णविहीनसमं
यदि कारणकार्यविहीनसमम् ।
यदि भेदविभेदविहीनसमं
किमु रोदिषि मानसि सर्वसमम् ॥

yadi varṇa-vivarṇa-vihīna-samaṁ
yadi kāraṇa-kārya-vihīna-samam,
yadi bheda-vibheda-vihīna-samaṁ
kimu rodiṣi mānasi sarva-samam.

When Free of Caste and Castelessness, You are the Same,
When Free of Cause and Effect, You are the Same,
When Free of Division and Nondivision, You are the Same,
Then why do you sorrow O Mind,
You are the One Singular Truth of All Existence.

5.21

इह सर्वनिरन्तरसर्वचिते
इह केवलनिश्चलसर्वचिते ।
द्विपदादिविवर्जितसर्वचिते
किमु रोदिषि मानसि सर्वसमम् ॥

iha sarva-nirantara-sarva-cite
iha kevala-niścala-sarva-cite,
dvipadādi-vivarjita-sarva-cite
kimu rodiṣi mānasi sarva-samam.

It is the Eternal Self in all, It is the Consciousness in all.
It is the One Unchanging Self, It is the Consciousness in all.
Free of men and beings, It is the Consciousness in all.
Then why do you sorrow O Mind,
You are the One Singular Truth of All Existence.

5.22

अतिसर्वनिरन्तरसर्वगतं
अतिनिर्मलनिश्चलसर्वगतम् ।
दिनरात्रिविवर्जितसर्वगतं
किमु रोदिषि मानसि सर्वसमम् ॥

ati-sarva-nirantara-sarva-gataṁ
ati-nirmala-niścala-sarva-gatam,
dina-rātri-vivarjita-sarva-gataṁ
kimu rodiṣi mānasi sarva-samam.

It is the Ever Eternal Self in All, and All-Pervading.
It is of Pristine Purity, Unchanging, and All-Pervading.
Beyond day and night, It is All-Pervading.
Then why do you sorrow O Mind,
You are the One Singular Truth of All Existence.

5.23

न हि बन्धविबन्धसमागमनं
न हि योगवियोगसमागमनम् ।
न हि तर्कवितर्कसमागमनं
किमु रोदिषि मानसि सर्वसमम् ॥

na hi bandha-vibandha-samāgamanaṁ
na hi yoga-viyoga-samāgamanam,
na hi tarka-vitarka-samāgamanaṁ
kimu rodiṣi mānasi sarva-samam.

Neither Bound nor Free, It is One and Entire.
Neither United nor Separated, It is One and Entire.
Neither Reasoning nor Argument, It is One and Entire.
Then why do you sorrow O Mind,
You are the One Singular Truth of All Existence.

5.24

इह कालविकालनिराकरणं
अणुमात्रकृशानुनिराकरणम् ।
न हि केवलसत्यनिराकरणं
किमु रोदिषि मानसि सर्वसमम् ॥

iha kāla-vikāla-nirākaraṇaṁ
aṇu-mātra-kṛsānu-nirākaraṇam,
na hi kevala-satya-nirākaraṇaṁ
kimu rodiṣi mānasi sarva-samam.

Here Time and Timelessness do not exist.
Atoms and Elements like fire, do not exist.
Only Truth never ceases to exist.
Then why do you sorrow O Mind,
You are the One Singular Truth of All Existence.

5.25

इह देहविदेहविहीन इति
ननु स्वप्नसुषुप्तिविहीनपरम् ।
अभिधानविधानविहीनपरं
किमु रोदिषि मानसि सर्वसमम् ॥

iha deha-videha-vihīna iti
nanu swapna-suṣupti-vihīna-param,
abhidhāna-vidhāna-vihīna-paraṁ
kimu rodiṣi mānasi sarva-samam.

The Supreme One is beyond Body and Bodilessness.
Undoubtedly beyond Dream and Sleep,
Naming and Using.
Then why do you sorrow O Mind,
You are the One Singular Truth of All Existence.

5.26

गगनोपमशुद्धविशालसमं
अतिसर्वविवर्जितसर्वसमम् ।
गतसारविसारविकारसमं
किमु रोदिषि मानसि सर्वसमम् ॥

gaganopama-śuddha-viśāla-samaṁ
ati-sarva-vivarjita-sarva-samam,
gata-sāra-visāra-vikāra-samaṁ
kimu rodiṣi mānasi sarva-samam.

It is All-Pervading like the Sky,
Pure, Vast, and the Same Everywhere.
Completely transcending all,
It is the Same Self in all.
Beyond Essence, Non-Essence and Modification,
It is the Same Self in all.
Then why do you sorrow O Mind,
You are the One Singular Truth of All Existence.

5.27

इह धर्मविधर्मविरागतर-
मिह वस्तुविवस्तुविरागतरम् ।
इह कामविकामविरागतरं
किमु रोदिषि मानसि सर्वसमम् ॥

iha dharma-vidharma-virāga-taram
iha vastu-vivastu-virāga-taram,
iha kāma-vikāma-virāga-taraṁ
kimu rodiṣi mānasi sarva-samam.

It is indifferent to Virtue and Vice.
It is indifferent to Objects and Non-Objects.
It is indifferent to Desire and Desirelessness.
Then why do you sorrow O Mind,
You are the One Singular Truth of All Existence.

5.28

सुखदुःखविवर्जितसर्वसम-
मिह शोकविशोकविहीनपरम् ।
गुरुशिष्यविवर्जिततत्त्वपरं
किमु रोदिषि मानसि सर्वसमम् ॥

sukha-duḥkha-vivarjita-sarva-samam
iha śoka-viśoka-vihīna-param,
guru-śiṣya-vivarjita-tattva-paraṁ
kimu rodiṣi mānasi sarva-samam.

Beyond Pleasure and Pain, It is the Same Self in All.
Beyond Grief and Elation, It is The Supreme.
Beyond Guru and Disciple, It is The Supreme Truth.
Then why do you sorrow O Mind,
You are the One Singular Truth of All Existence.

5.29

न किलाङ्कुरसारविसार इति
न चलाचलसाम्यविसाम्यमिति ।
अविचारविचारविहीनमिति
किमु रोदिषि मानसि सर्वसमम् ॥

na kilāṅkura-sāra-visāra iti
na calācala-sāmya-visāmyam-iti,
avicāra-vicāra-vihīnam-iti
kimu rodiṣi mānasi sarva-samam.

There is not even a trace of Essence or Non-Essence.
It is beyond Animate and Inanimate, Equality and Inequality,
Confusion and Discrimination.
Then why do you sorrow O Mind,
You are the One Singular Truth of All Existence.

5.30

इह सारसमुच्चयसारमिति
कथितं निजभावविभेद इति ।
विषये करणत्वमसत्यमिति
किमु रोदिषि मानसि सर्वसमम् ॥

iha sāra-samuccaya-sāram-iti
kathitaṁ nijabhāva-vibheda iti,
viṣaye karaṇatvam-asatyam-iti
kimu rodiṣi mānasi sarva-samam.

This Self is the Essence – the Essence of the Totality,
Said to be different from Individual Consciousness.
The notion that it is the Instrument of Perception is untrue.
Then why do you sorrow O Mind,
You are the One Singular Truth of All Existence.

5.31

बहुधा श्रुतयः प्रवदन्ति यतो
वियदादिरिदं मृगतोयसमम् ।
यदि चैकनिरन्तरसर्वसमं
किमु रोदिषि मानसि सर्वसमम् ॥

bahudhā śrutayaḥ pravadanti yato
viyadādir-idaṁ mṛga-toya-samam,
yadi caika-nirantara-sarva-samaṁ
kimu rodiṣi mānasi sarva-samam.

Scripture has said it in many ways,
This Universe of ether and other elements
Is like the Waters in a Mirage.
When there is the Same Self in all,
Then why do you sorrow O Mind,
You are the One Singular Truth of All Existence.

5.32

विन्दति विन्दति न हि न हि यत्र
छन्दोलक्षणं न हि न हि तत्र ।
समरसमग्नो भावितपूतः
प्रलपति तत्त्वं परमवधूतः ॥

vindati vindati na hi na hi yatra
chando-lakṣaṇaṁ na hi na hi tatra,
samarasa-magno bhāvita-pūtaḥ
pralapati tattvaṁ param-avadhūtaḥ.

Where there is no Knowing
There can be no Verses.
Purified by Meditation,
Deeply absorbed in Absolute Equanimity,
The Avadhūta has spoken the Supreme Truth.

Chapter 6

There is No Distinction between Cause and Effect

6.1

बहुधा श्रुतयः प्रवदन्ति वयं
वियदादिरिदं मृगतोयसमम् ।
यदि चैकनिरन्तरसर्वशिव-
मुपमेयमथोह्युपमा च कथम् ॥

bahudhā śrutayaḥ pravadanti vayaṁ
viyadādir-idaṁ mṛga-toya-samam,
yadi caika-nirantara-sarva-śivam
upameyam-atho-hyupamā ca katham.

Scripture has said it in many ways,
This Universe of Space and other elements
Is like the Waters in a Mirage.
If there is Only the One Indivisible Truth in All,
How then, can one Compare It, and to What?

6.2

अविभक्तिविभक्तिविहीनपरं
ननु कार्यविकार्यविहीनपरम् ।
यदि चैकनिरन्तरसर्वशिवं
यजनं च कथं तपनं च कथम् ॥

avibhakti-vibhakti-vihīna-paraṁ
nanu kārya-vikārya-vihīna-param,
yadi caika-nirantara-sarva-śivaṁ
yajanaṁ ca kathaṁ tapanaṁ ca katham.

The Absolute is beyond Non-Division and Division.
The Absolute is truly beyond Action and Alteration.
If there is Only the One Indivisible Truth in All,
How then, can one perform Sacrifice and Austerity?

6.3

मन एव निरन्तरसर्वगतं
ह्यविशालविशालविहीनपरम् ।
मन एव निरन्तरसर्वशिवं
मनसापि कथं वचसा च कथम् ॥

mana eva nirantara-sarva-gataṁ
hyaviśāla-viśāla-vihīna-param,
mana eva nirantara-sarva-śivaṁ
manasāpi kathaṁ vacasā ca katham.

The Self is truly Indivisible and All-Pervasive.
It is the Supreme - beyond Vastness and Smallness.
The Self is the Indivisible Truth in All.
How then, can It be Conceived or Articulated?

6.4

दिनरात्रिविभेदनिराकरण-
मुदितानुदितस्य निराकरणम् ।
यदि चैकनिरन्तरसर्वशिवं
रविचन्द्रमसौ ज्वलनश्च कथम् ॥

dina-rātri-vibheda-nirākaraṇam
uditānuditasya nirākaraṇam,
yadi caika-nirantara-sarva-śivaṁ
ravi-candramasau jvalanaś-ca katham.

The differentiation of Day and Night is denied in It.
The differentiation of Sunrise and Sunset is denied in It.
When there is Only the One Indivisible Truth in All,
How then, can there be the Sun, the Moon, and the Fire?

6.5

गतकामविकामविभेद इति
गतचेष्टविचेष्टविभेद इति ।
यदि चैकनिरन्तरसर्वशिवं
बहिरन्तरभिन्नमतिश्च कथम् ॥

gata-kāma-vikāma-vibheda iti
gata-ceṣṭa-vi-ceṣṭa-vibheda iti,
yadi caika-nirantara-sarva-śivaṁ
bahir-antara bhinna-matiś-ca katham.

Beyond the differentiation of Desire and Desirelessness,
Beyond the differentiation of Action and Inaction,
When there is Only the One Indivisible Truth in All,
How then, can there be the notion of Outside and Inside?

6.6

यदि सारविसारविहीन इति
यदि शून्यविशून्यविहीन इति ।
यदि चैकनिरन्तरसर्वशिवं
प्रथमं च कथं चरमं च कथम् ॥

yadi sāra-visāra-vihīna iti
yadi śūnya-viśūnya-vihīna iti,
yadi caika-nirantara-sarva-śivaṁ
prathamaṁ ca kathaṁ caramaṁ ca katham.

When It has transcended both Essence and Non-Essence,
When It has transcended both Emptiness and Fullness,
When there is Only the One Indivisible Truth in All,
How then, can there be an Initial?
How then, can there be a Final?

6.7

यदिभेदविभेदनिराकरणं
यदि वेदकवेद्यनिराकरणम् ।
यदि चैकनिरन्तरसर्वशिवं
तृतीयं च कथं तुरीयं च कथम् ॥

yadi-bheda-vibheda-nirākaraṇaṁ
yadi vedaka-vedya-nirākaraṇam,
yadi caika-nirantara sarva-śivaṁ
tritīyaṁ ca kathaṁ turīyaṁ ca katham.

When Division and Non-Division are denied,
When Knower and Known are denied,
When there is Only the One Indivisible Truth in All,
How then, can there be the Third (sleep)?
How then, can there be the Fourth (samadhi)?

6.8

गदिताविदितं न हि सत्यमिति
विदिताविदितं न हि सत्यमिति ।
यदि चैकनिरन्तरसर्वशिवं
विषयेन्द्रियबुद्धिमनांसि कथम् ॥

gaditāviditaṁ na hi satyam-iti
viditāviditaṁ na hi satyam-iti,
yadi caika-nirantara-sarva-śivaṁ
viṣayendriya-buddhi-manāṁsi katham.

The Spoken and the Unspoken Word are not the Truth.
The Known and the Unknown are not the Truth.
When there is Only the One Indivisible Truth in All,
How can there be Objects, Senses, Intellect, or Mind?

6.9

गगनं पवनो न हि सत्यमिति
धरणी दहनो न हि सत्यमिति ।
यदि चैकनिरन्तरसर्वशिवं
जलदश्च कथं सलिलं च कथम् ॥

gaganaṁ pavano na hi satyam-iti
dharaṇī dahano na hi satyam-iti,
yadi caika-nirantara-sarva-śivaṁ
jaladaś-ca kathaṁ salilaṁ ca katham.

Space and Air are not the Truth.
Earth and Fire are not the Truth.
When there is Only the One Indivisible Truth in All,
How can there be Clouds?
How can there be Water?

6.10

यदि कल्पितलोकनिराकरणं
यदि कल्पितदेवनिराकरणम् ।
यदि चैकनिरन्तरसर्वशिवं
गुणदोषविचारमतिश्च कथम् ॥

yadi kalpita-loka-nirākaraṇaṁ
yadi kalpita-deva-nirākaraṇam,
yadi caika-nirantara-sarva-śivaṁ
guṇa-doṣa-vicāra-matiś-ca katham.

When Imagined Worlds are Rejected,
When Imagined Gods are Rejected,
When there is Only the One Indivisible Truth in All,
How can there be the notion of Good and Evil?

6.11

मरणामरणं हि निराकरणं
करणाकरणं हि निराकरणम् ।
यदि चैकनिरन्तरसर्वशिवं
गमनागमनं हि कथं वदति ॥

maraṇāmaraṇaṁ hi nirākaraṇaṁ
karaṇākaraṇaṁ hi nirākaraṇam,
yadi caika-nirantara-sarva-śivaṁ
gamanāgamanaṁ hi kathaṁ vadati.

Death and Deathlessness are denied.
Action and Inaction are denied.
When there is Only the One Indivisible Truth in All,
How can one speak of Coming and Going?

6.12

प्रकृतिः पुरुषो न हि भेद इति
न हि कारणकार्यविभेद इति ।
यदि चैकनिरन्तरसर्वशिवं
पुरुषापुरुषं च कथं वदति ॥

prakṛtiḥ puruṣo na hi bheda iti
na hi kāraṇa-kārya-vibheda iti,
yadi caika-nirantara-sarva-śivaṁ
puruṣāpuruṣaṁ ca kathaṁ vadati.

There is no distinction between Prakriti and Puruṣa.
There is no distinction between Cause and Effect.
When there is Only the One Indivisible Truth in All,
How can one speak of Self and not-Self?

6.13

तृतीयं न हि दुःखसमागमनं
न गुणाद्द्वितीयस्य समागमनम् ।
यदि चैकनिरन्तरसर्वशिवं
स्थविरश्च युवा च शिशुश्च कथम् ॥

tritīyaṁ na hi duḥkha samāgamanaṁ
na guṇād-dvitīyasya samāgamanam,
yadi caika-nirantara-sarva-śivaṁ
sthaviraś-ca yuvā ca śiśuś-ca katham.

In It, there is not the Misery of Old Age,
Nor the Joy of Youth.
When there is Only the One Indivisible Truth in All,
How can there be Old Age, Youth, and Childhood?

6.14

ननु आश्रमवर्णविहीनपरं
ननु कारणकर्तृविहीनपरम् ।
यदि चैकनिरन्तरसर्वशिव-
मविनष्टविनष्टमतिश्च कथम् ॥

nanu āśrama-varṇa-vihīna-paraṁ
nanu kāraṇa-kartṛ-vihīna-param,
yadi caika-nirantara-sarva-śivam
avinaṣṭa-vinaṣṭa-matiś-ca katham.

Undoubtedly, the Supreme is devoid of Caste and Stages of Life.
Undoubtedly, the Supreme is devoid of Cause and Agency.
When there is Only the One Indivisible Truth in All,
How can there be the notion of Non-Destruction or Destruction?

6.15

ग्रसिताग्रसितं च वितथ्यमिति
जनिताजनितं च वितथ्यमिति ।
यदि चैकनिरन्तरसर्वशिव-
मविनाशि विनाशि कथं हि भवेत् ॥

grasitāgrasitaṁ ca vitathyam-iti
janitājanitaṁ ca vitathyam-iti,
yadi caika-nirantara-sarva-śivam
avināśi vināśi kathaṁ hi bhavet.

The Destroyed and the Undestroyed are false notions.
The Born and the Unborn are false notions.
When there is Only the One Indivisible Truth in All,
How can there be the Immortal or the Mortal?

6.16

पुरुषापुरुषस्य विनष्टमिति
वनितावनितस्य विनष्टमिति ।
यदि चैकनिरन्तरसर्वशिव-
मविनोदविनोदमतिश्च कथम् ॥

puruṣāpuruṣasya vinaṣṭam-iti
vanitāvanitasya vinaṣṭam-iti,
yadi caika-nirantara-sarva-śivam
avinoda-vinoda-matiś-ca katham.

Notions of Masculine and Non-Masculine disappear.
Notions of Feminine and Non-Feminine disappear.
When there is Only the One Indivisible Truth in All,
How can there be the notion of Boredom or Amusement?

6.17

यदि मोहविषादविहीनपरो
यदि संशयशोकविहीनपरः ।
यदि चैकनिरन्तरसर्वशिव-
महमेति ममेति कथं च पुनः ॥

yadi moha-viṣāda-vihīna-paro
yadi samśaya-śoka-vihīna-paraḥ,
yadi caika-nirantara-sarva-śivam
aham-eti mameti kathaṁ ca punaḥ.

When the Supreme is free of Delusion and Melancholia,
When the Supreme is free of Doubt and Sorrow,
When there is Only the One Indivisible Truth in All,
How then can there be I or mine?

6.18

ननु धर्मविधर्मविनाश इति
ननु बन्धविबन्धविनाश इति ।
यदि चैकनिरन्तरसर्वशिव-
मिहदुःखविदुःखमतिश्च कथम् ॥

nanu dharma-vidharma-vināśa iti
nanu bandha-vibandha-vināśa iti,
yadi caika-nirantara-sarva-śivam
iha-duḥkha-viduḥkha-matiś-ca katham.

Undoubtedly Virtue and Vice are destroyed.
Undoubtedly Bondage and Freedom are destroyed.
When there is Only the One Indivisible Truth in All,
How can there be the notion of Sorrow or the Absence of Sorrow?

6.19

न हि याज्ञिकयज्ञविभाग इति
न हुताशनवस्तुविभाग इति ।
यदि चैकनिरन्तरसर्वशिवं
वद कर्मफलानि भवन्ति कथम् ॥

na hi yājñika-yajña-vibhāga iti
na hutāśana-vastu-vibhāga iti,
yadi caika-nirantara-sarva-śivaṁ
vada karma-phalāni bhavanti katham.

No distinction lies between the Performer and the Sacrifice.
No distinction lies between the Fire and the Offerings.
When there is Only the One Indivisible Truth in All,
How can there be the Fruit of Action?

6.20

ननु शोकविशोकविमुक्त इति
ननु दर्पविदर्पविमुक्त इति ।
यदि चैकनिरन्तरसर्वशिवं
ननु रागविरागमतिश्च कथम् ॥

nanu śoka-viśoka-vimukta iti
nanu darpa-vidarpa-vimukta iti,
yadi caika-nirantara-sarva-śivaṁ
nanu rāga-virāga-matiś-ca katham.

Undoubtedly, It is free of Sorrow and the Absence of Sorrow.
Undoubtedly, It is free of Pride and the Absence of Pride.
When there is Only the One Indivisible Truth in All,
How can there be the notion of Passion and Dispassion?

6.21

न हि मोहविमोहविकार इति
न हि लोभविलोभविकार इति ।
यदि चैकनिरन्तरसर्वशिवं
ह्यविवेकविवेकमतिश्च कथम् ॥

na hi moha-vimoha-vikāra iti
na hi lobha-vilobha-vikāra iti,
yadi caika-nirantara-sarva-śivaṁ
hyaviveka-viveka-matiś-ca katham.

There is no such deviation as Delusion or Non-Delusion.
There is no such deviation as Greed or Non-Greed.
When there is Only the One Indivisible Truth in All,
How can there be the notion of Non-Discrimination or Discrimination?

6.22

त्वमहं न हि हन्त कदाचिदपि
कुलजातिविचारमसत्यमिति ।
अहमेव शिवः परमार्थ इति
अभिवादनमत्र करोमि कथम् ॥

twam-ahaṁ na hi hanta kadācid-api
kula-jāti-vicāram-asatyam-iti,
aham-eva śivaḥ paramārtha iti
abhivādanam-atra karomi katham.

You and I have Never Existed!
Notions of Family and Caste are Untrue.
Truly, I am the Truth, the Supreme Reality.
How, in what manner then, should I offer Devotion?

6.23

गुरुशिष्यविचारविशीर्ण इति
उपदेशविचारविशीर्ण इति ।
अहमेव शिवः परमार्थ इति
अभिवादनमत्र करोमि कथम् ॥

guru-śiṣya-vicāra-viśīrṇa iti
upadeśa-vicāra-viśīrṇa iti,
aham-eva śivaḥ paramārtha iti
abhivādanam-atra karomi katham.

The notion of Teacher and Disciple is destroyed.
The notion of Instruction is destroyed.
Truly, I am the Truth, the Supreme Reality.
How, in what manner then, should I offer Devotion?

6.24

न हि कल्पितदेहविभाग इति
न हि कल्पितलोकविभाग इति ।
अहमेव शिवः परमार्थ इति
अभिवादनमत्र करोमि कथम् ॥

na hi kalpita-deha-vibhāga iti
na hi kalpita-loka-vibhāga iti,
aham-eva śivaḥ paramārtha iti
abhivādanam-atra karomi katham.

There are no Imaginary Individual Bodies.
There are no Imaginary Individual Worlds.
Truly, I am the Truth, the Supreme Reality.
How, in what manner then, should I offer Devotion?

6.25

सरजो विरजो न कदाचिदपि
ननु निर्मलनिश्चलशुद्ध इति ।
अहमेव शिवः परमार्थ इति
अभिवादनमत्र करोमि कथम् ॥

sarajo virajo na kadācid-api
nanu nirmala-niścala-śuddha iti,
aham-eva śivaḥ paramārtha iti
abhivādanam-atra karomi katham.

Ever free of Passion and Dispassion,
Undoubtedly Unsullied, Immovable and Pure.
Truly, I am the Truth, the Supreme Reality.
How, in what manner then, should I offer Devotion?

6.26

न हि देहविदेहविकल्प इति
अनृतं चरितं न हि सत्यमिति ।
अहमेव शिवः परमार्थ इति
अभिवादनमत्र करोमि कथम् ॥

na hi deha-videha-vikalpa iti
anṛitaṁ caritaṁ na hi satyam-iti,
aham-eva śivaḥ paramārtha iti
abhivādanam-atra karomi katham.

The distinction between Body and Bodilessness does not exist.
False Action does not exist.
Truly, I am the Truth, the Supreme Reality.
How, in what manner then, should I offer Devotion?

6.27

विन्दति विन्दति न हि न हि यत्र
छन्दोलक्षणं न हि न हि तत्र ।
समरसमग्नो भावितपूतः
प्रलपति तत्त्वं परमवधूतः ॥

vindati vindati na hi na hi yatra
chando-lakṣaṇaṁ na hi na hi tatra,
samarasa-magno bhāvita-pūtaḥ
pralapati tattvaṁ param-avadhūtaḥ.

Where there is no Knowing
There can be no Verses.
Purified by Meditation,
Deeply absorbed in Absolute Equanimity,
The Avadhūta has spoken the Supreme Truth.

Chapter 7

He is the Absolute – Pure and Perfect

7.1

रथ्याकर्पटविरचितकन्थः
पुण्यापुण्यविवर्जितपन्थः ।
शून्यागारे तिष्ठति नग्नो
शुद्धनिरञ्जनसमरसमग्नः ॥

rathyā-karpaṭa-virachita-kanthaḥ
puṇyāpuṇya-vivarjita-panthaḥ,
śūnyāgāre tiṣṭhati nagno
śuddha-nirañjana-samarasa-magnaḥ.

Wearing old patched rags from the streets,
He follows the path beyond virtue and vice.
Dwelling disrobed in a deserted place,
He lives - Pure, Sinless, absorbed in Bliss.

7.2

लक्ष्यालक्ष्यविवर्जितलक्ष्यो
युक्तायुक्तविवर्जितदक्षः ।
केवलतत्त्वनिरञ्जनपूतो
वादविवादः कथमवधूतः ॥

lakṣyālakṣya-vivarjita-lakṣyo
yuktāyukta-vivarjita-dakṣaḥ,
kevala-tattva-nirañjana-pūtaḥ
vādavivādaḥ katham-avadhūtaḥ.

His Purpose is beyond Purpose and Purposelessness.
His Disposition, beyond Proper and Improper.
He is the Absolute Truth, Perfect and Pure.
How then can the Avadhuta engage in argument?

7.3

आशापाशविबन्धनमुक्ताः
शौचाचारविवर्जितयुक्ताः ।
एवं सर्वविवर्जितशान्त-
स्तत्त्वं शुद्धनिरञ्जनवन्तः ॥

āśā-pāśa-vibandhana-muktāḥ
śaucācāra-vivarjita-yuktāḥ,
evam sarva-vivarjita-śāntaḥ
tattvaṁ śuddha-nirañjanavantaḥ.

Free of Bondage from the Chains of Hope,
Free of the Norms of Conduct, Absorbed in the Self,
Free of Everything, and Serene,
He is the Absolute - Pure and Perfect.

7.4

कथमिह देहविदेहविचारः
कथमिह रागविरागविचारः ।
निर्मलनिश्चलगगनाकारं
स्वयमिह तत्त्वं सहजाकारम् ॥

katham-iha deha-videha-vicāraḥ
katham-iha rāga-virāga-vicāraḥ,
nirmala-niścala-gaganākāraṁ
swayam-iha tattvaṁ sahajākāram.

How can there be a query about Body or No Body?
How can there be a query about Attachment or no Attachment?
Pure, Unchangeable, Infinite as Space,
He is the Truth – the Innate Reality.

7.5

कथमिह तत्त्वं विन्दति यत्र
रूपमरूपं कथमिह तत्र ।
गगनाकारः परमो यत्र
विषयीकरणं कथमिह तत्र ॥

katham-iha tattvaṁ vindati yatra
rūpam-arūpaṁ katham-iha tatra,
gaganākāraḥ paramo yatra
viṣayikaraṇaṁ katham-iha tatra.

In the State of Awareness, how can there be Knowing?
In the State of Awareness, how can there be Form or Formlessness?
When the Supreme is Formless like the Sky,
How can there be the differentiation of Objects?

7.6

गगनाकारनिरन्तरहंस-
स्तत्त्वविशुद्धनिरञ्जनहंसः ।
एवं कथमिह भिन्नविभिन्नं
बन्धविबन्धविकारविभिन्नम् ॥

gaganākara-nirantara-hamsaḥ
tattva-viśuddha-nirañjana-hamsaḥ,
evam katham-iha bhinna-vibhinnaṁ
bandha-vibandha-vikāra-vibhinnam.

The Supreme Self is Entire and Infinite like Space.
The Supreme Self is the Absolute Truth, Pure and Immaculate.
How then can there be Difference or Non-Difference,
Bondage or Freedom, Distortion or Variance?

7.7

केवलतत्त्वनिरन्तरसर्वं
योगवियोगौ कथमिह गर्वम् ।
एवं परमनिरन्तरसर्व-
मेवं कथमिह सारविसारम् ॥

kevala-tattva-nirantara-sarvaṁ
yoga-viyogau katham-iha garvam,
evaṁ parama-nirantara-sarvam
evaṁ katham-iha sāra-visāram.

The One Absolute Truth is All and Entire,
How then can there be Union or Separation or Pride?
Truly the Supreme is All and Entire,
How then can there be Essence and Non-Essence?

7.8

केवलतत्त्वनिरञ्जनसर्वं
गगनाकारनिरन्तरशुद्धम् ।
एवं कथमिह सङ्गविसङ्गं
सत्यं कथमिह रङ्गविरङ्गम् ॥

kevala-tattva-nirañjana-sarvaṁ
gaganākāra-nirantara-śuddham,
evam katham-iha saṅga-visaṅgaṁ
satyam katham-iha raṅga-viraṅgam.

The One Absolute Truth is Pure and Whole,
Infinite like Space, Eternal, and Pristine.
How then can there be Togetherness or Separateness?
Truly, how then can there be Revelry or Sobriety?

7.9

योगवियोगै रहितो योगी
भोगविभोगै रहितो भोगी ।
एवं चरति हि मन्दं मन्दं
मनसा कल्पितसहजानन्दम् ॥

yoga-viyogaiḥ rahito yogī
bhoga-vibhogaiḥ rahito bhogī,
evaṁ carati hi mandaṁ mandaṁ
manasā kalpita-sahajānandam.

Transcending Union and Separation, he is a Yogi.
Transcending Enjoyment and Non-Enjoyment, he is an Enjoyer.
He walks languorously at his leisure,
His mind enjoying the Bliss of the Self.

7.10

बोधविबोधैः सततं युक्तो
द्वैताद्वैतैः कथमिह मुक्तः ।
सहजो विरजः कथमिह योगी
शुद्धनिरञ्जनसमरसभोगी ॥

bodha-vibodhaiḥ satatam̐ yukto
dvaitādvaitaiḥ katham-iha muktaḥ,
sahajo virajaḥ katham-iha yogī
śuddha-nirañjana-samarasa-bhogī.

How can one who is consumed
With Knowledge and Ignorance, Duality and Non-Duality,
Be regarded as Liberated?
How can Simpleness and Desirelessness define a Yogi-
He, who is Pure, Unblemished, and the enjoyer of Bliss?

7.11

भग्नाभग्नविवर्जितभग्नो
लग्नालग्नविवर्जितलग्नः ।
एवं कथमिह सारविसारः
समरसतत्त्वं गगनाकारः ॥

bhagnābhagna-vivarjita-bhagno
lagnālagna-vivarjita-lagnaḥ,
evaṁ katham-iha sāra-visāraḥ
samarasa-tattvaṁ gaganākāraḥ.

Neither Divided nor Undivided, It is free of Division.
Neither Attached nor Unattached, It is free of Attachment.
How can It be the Essence or the Non-Essence
When it is Bliss and Truth, Formless like the Sky?

7.12

सततं सर्वविवर्जितयुक्तः
सर्वं तत्त्वविवर्जितमुक्तः ।
एवं कथमिह जीवितमरणं
ध्यानाध्यानैः कथमिह करणम् ॥

satataṁ sarva-vivarjita-yuktaḥ
sarvaṁ tattva-vivarjita-muktaḥ,
evaṁ katham-iha jīvita-maraṇaṁ
dhyānādhyanaiḥ katham-iha karaṇam.

Eternally Free of Everything, yet One with Everything,
Transcending Everything, he is Liberated.
How then, can there be Life or Death for him?
How can there be Meditation or No Meditation for him?

7.13

इन्द्रजालमिदं सर्वं यथा मरुमरीचिका ।
अखण्डितमनाकारो वर्तते केवलः शिवः ॥

indrajālam-idaṁ sarvaṁ yathā maru-marīcika,
akhaṇḍitam-anākāro vartate kevalaḥ śivaḥ.

All this is Illusion
Like the Waters in a Mirage.
Only the Absolute Truth Exists,
Indivisible and Formless.

7.14

धर्मादौ मोक्षपर्यन्तं निरीहाः सर्वथा वयम् ।
कथं रागविरागैश्च कल्पयन्ति विपश्चितः ॥

dharmādau mokṣa-paryantaṁ nirīhaḥ sarvathā vayam,
kathaṁ rāga-virāgaiś-ca kalpayanti vipaścitaḥ.

We are Indifferent to Everything
From Religious Duties to Liberation.
How then can we have Attachment or Detachment,
That is the Imagination of the Learned.

7.15

विन्दति विन्दति न हि न हि यत्र
छन्दोलक्षणं न हि न हि तत्र ।
समरसमग्नो भावितपूतः
प्रलपति तत्त्वं परमवधूतः ॥

vindati vindati na hi na hi yatra
chando-lakṣaṇaṁ na hi na hi tatra,
samarasa-magno bhāvita-pūtaḥ
pralapati tattvaṁ param-avadhūtaḥ.

Where there is no Knowing
There can be no Verses.
Purified by Meditation,
Deeply absorbed in Absolute Equanimity,
The Avadhūta has spoken the Supreme Truth.

Chapter 8

He lives in A State of Eternal Bliss

8.1

त्वद्यात्रया व्यापकता हता ते
ध्यानेन चेतःपरता हता ते ।
स्तुत्या मया वाक्परता हता ते
क्षमस्व नित्यं त्रिविधापराधान् ॥

tvad-yātrayā vyāpakatā hatā te
dhyānena cetaḥ-paratā hatā te,
stutyā mayā vākparatā hatā te
kṣamasva nityaṁ trividhāparādhān.

My Pilgrimage to You
Has disregarded your Omnipresence.
My Meditation on You
Has disregarded your Transcendence of Mind.
My Praise of You
Has disregarded your Transcendence of Speech.
Ever Forgive me my three Misdeeds.

8.2

कामैरहतधीर्दान्तो मृदुः शुचिरकिञ्चनः ।
अनीहो मितभुक् शान्तः स्थिरो मच्छरणो मुनिः ॥

kāmai-rahat-adhīr-dānto mṛduḥ śucir-akiñcanaḥ,
anīho mita-bhuk śāntaḥ sthiro maccharaṇo muniḥ.

He who is Free of Desire, Restrained,
Amiable, Pure, Free of Possessions,
Indifferent, Not Covetous, Reposeful, Resolute,
And has taken refuge in the Self, is a Muni.

8.3

अप्रमत्तो गभीरात्मा धृतिमान् जितषड्गुणः ।
अमानी मानदः कल्पो मैत्रः कारुणिकः कविः ॥

apramatto gabhīrātmā dhṛtimān jita-ṣaḍ-guṇaḥ,
amānī mānadaḥ kalpo maitraḥ kāruṇikaḥ kaviḥ.

The Sage is Attentive, Profound, and Calm,
Subjugator of the five Senses and Mind,
Modest, Respectful, and Proper,
Friendly, Compassionate, and Deeply Insightful.

8.4

कृपालुरकृतद्रोहस्तितिक्षुः सर्वदेहिनाम् ।
सत्यसारोऽनवद्यात्मा समः सर्वोपकारकः ॥

kṛpālurakṛta-drohaḥ-titikṣuḥ sarva-dehinām,
satya-sāro-anavadyātmā samaḥ sarvopakārakaḥ.

The Sage is Merciful, Nonviolent,
Forbearing towards all living beings,
The Essence of Truth, Unsullied,
Same to All, and Beneficent to All.

8.5

अवधूतलक्षणं वर्णैर्ज्ञातव्यं भगवत्तमैः ।
वेदवर्णार्थतत्त्वज्ञैर्वेदवेदान्तवादिभिः ॥

avadhūta-lakṣaṇaṁ varṇaiḥ-jñātavyaṁ bhagavattamaiḥ,
veda-varṇārtha-tattvajñaiḥ-veda-vedānta-vādibhiḥ.

The traits of the Avadhūta,
And the meaning of the syllables,
Are known by the Blessed Ones,
Who know their Meaning and Essence,
And who are Teachers of the Vedas and Vedānta.

8.6

आशापाशविनिर्मुक्त आदिमध्यान्तनिर्मलः ।
आनन्दे वर्तते नित्यमकारं तस्य लक्षणम् ॥

āśā-pāśa-vinirmukta ādi-madhyānta-nir-malaḥ,
ānande vartate nityam-akāraṁ tasya lakṣaṇam.

The A in Avadhūta means,
One who is Free of the Chains of Hope (Āsha),
Whose Life is Pure in the Beginning, Middle, and End (Ādi, Madhya, Anta),
And who Lives in a State of Perpetual, Eternal Bliss (Ānanda).

8.7

वासना वर्जिता येन वक्तव्यं च निरामयम् ।
वर्तमानेषु वर्तेत वकारं तस्य लक्षणम् ॥

vāsanā varjitā yena vaktavyaṁ ca nirāmayam,
vartamāneṣu vartate vakāraṁ tasya lakṣaṇam.

The VA in Avadhūta means,
One who is Free of Desire (VĀsanā),
Whose Speech (VĀk) is Pure,
And who Lives in the Present (VArtamān).

8.8

धूलिधूसरगात्राणि धूतचित्तो निरामयः ।
धारणाध्याननिर्मुक्तो धूकारस्तस्य लक्षणम् ॥

dhūli-dhūsara-gātrāṇi dhūta-citto nirāmayaḥ,
dhāraṇā-dhyāna-nirmukto dhūkāras-tasya lakṣaṇam.

The DHŪ in Avadhūta means,
One whose Body is Grey with Dust (DHŪli),
Whose Mind is Pure (DHŪta-citto),
And who No Longer Needs to Meditate (DHāraṇā-DHyāna).

8.9

तत्त्वचिन्ता धृता येन चिन्ताचेष्टाविवर्जितः ।
तमोऽहंकारनिर्मुक्तस्तकारस्तस्य लक्षणम् ॥

tattva-cintā dhṛtā yena cintā-ceṣtā-vivarajitaḥ,
tamo'hankāra-nirmuktaḥ-takāras-tasya lakṣaṇam.

The TA in Avadhūta means,
One who is Absorbed in the Contemplation of Truth
(TAttva-cintā),
Who is Free of Anxiety and Action (cinTĀ -ceṣTĀ),
And who is Free of Ignorance and Egoism (TAmo'hankāra).

8.10

दत्तात्रेयावधूतेन निर्मितानन्दरूपिणा ।
ये पठन्ति च शृण्वन्ति तेषां नैव पुनर्भवः ॥

Dattātreya-avadhūtena nirmita -ānanda-rūpiṇā,
ye paṭhanti ca śṛṇvanti teṣāṁ naiva punarbhavaḥ.

This Song has been Composed by the Avadhūta Dattātreya,
Who is the Manifestation of Bliss.
Those who Read it or Hear it,
Are Freed from Rebirth.

Om Tat Sat

Other Books by the Same Author

Available on Amazon.com

Beyond The Word
A translation of
Aṣṭāvakra Saṁhitā
Anonymous

A Thousand Suns
A translation of
The Holy Gita
Petal

Printed in Great Britain
by Amazon

24674033R10169